The First Rites

The First Rites

Worship in the Early Church

Kenneth W. Stevenson

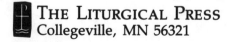 THE LITURGICAL PRESS
Collegeville, MN 56321

This book was first published in 1989 in the United Kingdom by Marshall Morgan and Scott Publications Ltd., part of the Marshall Pickering Holdings Group.

Copyright © 1989 by Kenneth W. Stevenson.

This edition by The Liturgical Press has been published for marketing in the United States of America and in Canada.

Cover design by Joshua Jeide, O.S.B.

1   2   3   4   5   6   7

Library of Congress Cataloging-in-Publication Data
Stevenson, Kenneth (Kenneth W.)
    The first rites : worship in the early church / Kenneth Stevenson.
      p.   cm.
    Includes bibliographical references.
    ISBN 0-8146-1951-7
    1. Liturgies, Early Christian.   I. Title.
BV185.S8   1989
264'01--dc20   89-78280
                                                     CIP

Contents

List of Illustrations

Preface

In spring 1988 I was invited to present three programs for BBC television on early Christian worship. In previous jobs, I had lectured on the history of worship to students at Lincoln Theological College and at the universities of Manchester and Notre Dame (USA). Now came my chance to reach a wider audience than I ever had before. The following pages are offered as a sort of extension of those programs for the more general reader who wants to get a picture of what it might have felt like to take part in various kinds of services as they emerged in the first three centuries. I have taken the necessary risk of oversimplifying, although I have made it clear time and again what sort of evidence it is that we have to use. To my mind, those first stages of the Christian era continue to be of vital importance. They have been far more formative on Christian worship down the ages than any of us realize.

My friends and colleagues may well recognize themselves in certain parts of the text. Any errors of fact or interpretation, however, are mine and mine alone. It has been fun to put it together! And I gladly dedicate this little offering to the international community of liturgy scholars, one of the friendliest in academe. I am also grateful to my father, the Reverend Eric Stevenson, for once again making needful illustrations in one of his son's productions. I hope they will convey that worship in any age is something to experience rather than just something you can read about.

Each chapter will deal with one specific type of service, approaching through the eyes of the twentieth century, problems and all. The evidence is set before the reader. Then some conclusions are offered, suggesting how we may learn a few lessons, or not, as the case may be. We ignore those crucial centuries at our peril. More to the point, they are enormously exciting.

Kenneth Stevenson
Guildford
Feast of the Transfiguration
6 August 1988

1: Introduction

(1)

Why bother to try to find how early Christians worshiped? When I used to teach the subject I was frequently asked this question, and I well remember the sort of reasons people used to give in order to stop me in my tracks. Here is a selection of them.

The first objection usually ran along the following lines. The early Christians were such a diverse group of people who came from so many different backgrounds and traditions that it simply isn't possible to find out very much about them. To put it bluntly—their worship is not *accessible* to us. We should, therefore, stick to our own business of worshiping in our own way because our forebears in those early centuries cannot really impinge on what we do.

The second objection is related to the first. It uses that magic word "irrelevant," and lays down the law that is above every other law, that how the early Christians worshiped is irrelevant to us because it doesn't mean anything to us. We who live in the twentieth century cannot afford to spend too much time on what might seem like a collection of old wives' tales. In our sophisticated environment, pluralist culture, and expanding knowledge of the universe the thought styles and language of our predecessors cannot possibly speak to us—other than in the bare facts themselves. At best they can inform us better, at worst they can fill us with outmoded liturgies, antiquated prayer-shapes, ancient documents.

The third objection really gets to the heart of the matter. It takes the firm line that even if one can find out how they worshiped and even if the study of the first Christian centuries can teach us one or two important facts, the result of the exercise cannot in any sense be *normative* on what we do today. By this is meant that beautiful and laudable as the study of antiquity may be in its own right, it really should be left to specialists (and perhaps left to them alone). How Christians broke bread in Syria or Rome at the start of the third century may be interesting in itself, but it *cannot* and *should not* be turned into some kind of norm for us in our day.

I want to explode these three myths in the course of this book not because I have some burning passion for antiquity (though that is true) but because I happen to think that each of these attitudes is very prevalent today—and each is (in my view) deeply misguided.

First of all, how early Christians worshiped *is accessible.* In the course of this book, we shall be looking again and again at documents that were carefully written down in the early centuries but which were sadly lost for many subsequent centuries. They thus ceased to have any influence on worship in the Middle Ages, and (most important of all) at the Reformation. This latter point is crucial to any discussion of liturgy, because the Reformers sought to purge the medieval worship that they had inherited of supposedly Catholic accretions. Had they had access to some of the texts we shall be looking at, we may well ask whether their liturgical work might have been more balanced, less wordy, and more deeply traditional.

Secondly, the argument from "relevance" is always a dangerous one because it smacks of the adolescent rebellion against anything that gets in the way. I have heard the word "irrelevant" used frequently in Christian circles, usually as a way of getting rid of something that people cannot be bothered to understand in the interests of some alleged freedom. I suspect that the "early Church is irrelevant" brigade secretly fear that if they were to take the trouble and find out how early Christians worshiped from the evidence that is available to us, they might have a nasty shock and discover one or two set forms, careful restraints placed on ministers by the community in the interests of remaining within a recognizable wider community. On the other hand, they may equally find other evidence to back up some of their hopes and fears against tradition for its own sake. How those early Christians, direct heirs to the New Testament, carried out their central cultic acts must be relevant to us because they grew out of the formative era of our religion. To study origins is a necessary and sobering exercise. And it changes and alters as a process as time goes on, because we return to them with fresh concerns. For example, a generation ago scholars who looked at those liturgies tended to harmonize differences in order to discern some more uniform picture. Nowadays, perhaps influenced by a desire to see the world in more pluriform terms, there is a tendency for scholars to look at both the differences and the similarities and to discern in them an important feature: that those differences amount to important local characteristics which tell us something important about the way Christians could remain in communion with one another but worship in slightly different ways.

Thirdly, to study the era of origins has to provide us with some basic norms in the sense that they challenge the way we worship today. To take a musical example, if some historians did not beaver away at the size and balance of orchestras at the time of Mozart, there would be no one to ask awkward questions of the "big band" enthusiasts, who insist that a symphony that may have been written for an orchestra that contained only a handful of violins might conceivably be savaged in performance if the first violins number around twenty.

This is not to suggest, of course, that all liturgies have to be ideologically sound and that we can only worship authentically if we are doing it in continuity with generations long since passed on. But it is to affirm that mere knowledge of how, for example, early Christians valued baptism ought to awaken sleepy Christians born again not of water and the Spirit but of secular consumerism to look once more at how Christian initiation is practiced in their locality. Of course, how the early Christians thought cannot, in some ways, be how we think. Everybody knows that the earth is not flat. But not everybody knows what riches are to be found in, for example, some early Christian Eucharistic prayers, which sometimes use the sort of simple, symbolic language that bypasses many of the doctrinal problems that festered through the Middle Ages and came to a head at the Reformation. We don't have to *imitate* the early centuries—but there can be little doubt that they propose to us certain significant norms that ought to challenge our own discipleship and the quality and depth of our worship.

(2)

But the issue goes deeper still. To say that the worship of antiquity is accessible, relevant, and, in some sense, normative is to take several steps along the road of our own self-understanding. *We* are the creatures of change, as our perceptions of ourselves and the world around us alter with the passage of time. If this book were to be written in a hundred years' time, it would be different in style and approach and (we may hope) in substance—provided that the next century yields some more important discoveries of ancient documents that may turn a few ideas on their head!

To make those assertions about the importance of early worship is to say crucial things about ourselves and our own needs. As Christians we are people with a story, and part of our own progress through history is to hold a continuing conversation with our roots. Today there is a growing sense of the importance of history coming through in the kinds of courses offered at educational institutes as well as the sort of programs that are now to be seen on television. Our own story gets fed as much in the way we appropriate our own past as in the way we use that in the present in order to construct the future.

History itself is full of surprises here. A hundred years ago it was fashionable in many church circles to look to the Middle Ages for a kind of golden age of architecture. This produced Gothic churches all over the country, like Doncaster Parish Church, clearly visible from the railway station. It also produced a cult of the medieval in secular architecture, hence a building like the House of Commons. Since then fashions have clearly changed! I detect, however, that there is a growing interest no longer in that great period of Christian efflorescence that made up the Middle Ages (even though thousands still flock to our cathedrals as tourists day by day) but rather in the period of our origins. This may be for a number of reasons.

First of all, the position of the Church in the Western world is by now very different from what it was a hundred years ago when the glories of medieval society somehow matched the bold self-confidence of Victorian Christianity. Christians are increasingly conscious of being at one and the same time a minority group in an alien society and also the purveyors of but one religion in a world that knows and admires many others. At the Lambeth Conference in 1988, the noisy bishops from the Old World got a jolt when they realized that there are now more black Anglican bishops than white ones. Moreover, when Nigerian bishops were questioned on the important issues facing their flocks, they said that the growing influence of Islam in its more fanatical form imposed enormous strains on local congregations, leading to frequent acts of violence and vandalism. But before that anecdote is dismissed for being a missionary tale, we should remember that there are many urban areas in England where Sikhs and Hindus as well as Jews far outnumber Christians, even at a most generous estimate of the Christian population.

To look, therefore, at another world, in which Christians were also a minority and in which they also made up a religious group that stood alongside many others, has an obvious attraction. We can compare and contrast our respective positions. We can see, for example, in the great changes that took place in the fourth century an oblique parallel to our own situation. In the fourth century the Church had to move out of smaller buildings and structures into much larger buildings where church life had to be more regimented simply because popularity brought larger numbers into the fold. Contrariwise, it could be suggested that in our own twentieth century the Western Churches are—in some sense—making the same move, but in reverse. We are trying to loosen up historic structures and much of our worship now is much more varied than it used to be. We see whole shapes of liturgies (rather than the individual words themselves) as the foundation of our community with each other. Perhaps to look at how the first Christians worshiped may provide us with a helpful parallel, even a mirror.

Secondly, we do now have much better knowledge of those first three centuries than we have ever had before. Even in the last hundred years our knowledge has increased to the extent that certain sources are now assured to us as reliable witnesses for our quest. (We shall list some of these shortly.) Being in such a position places us at an advantage, but it is important not to be swayed too much by a seeming *embarras de richesses*. Clearer as the picture may be than what it was a hundred years ago, it is still a picture dominated more by fog than clear air. And that is both its charm and its challenge.

For example, the illustration at the head of this chapter is one piece of chance architectural evidence. It depicts a house-church from the ancient city of Dura Europos in Syria, which lay on the right bank of the River Euphrates halfway between Aleppo and Baghdad. Most scholars are agreed that it dates from the third century. What is interesting about it is that, to all intents and purposes, it would have looked like any other patio-house from the

outside, but the main room is large enough to house a congregation of about forty and a separate room houses an impressive font.
Next door to it there was a small synagogue for the local Jewish
community. Here, on the edge of the Roman Empire, Christian
and Jew worshiped in geographical proximity. What the personal
relations between the two groups were like we are left to guess.
It is conceivable that the local authorities deliberately put them
side by side—or they may have ended up like that by accident.
Nonetheless, the house-church at Dura Europos supplies us with
important evidence of how a local congregation ordered itself:
a patio for social encounter, a large room for worship (including
the Eucharist), another room for baptisms (evidence that Christian initiation warranted a separate enclave), and yet another
room, perhaps for instructing those preparing for baptism. Different as our respective worlds are, many a contemporary Christian who worships today in a small brutalist worship center on
a housing estate has looked at the plan of this church community and seen more in common there than in an impressive
Romanesque basilica from medieval Germany.

Thirdly, one of the salient features of early Christianity is that
it survived persecution. We form an easy picture of someone like
Ignatius, who was bishop of Antioch at the turn of the first century and who was martyred under the terrible Emperor Trajan.
Escorted from Antioch to Rome, Ignatius refused any efforts to
have a reprieve, so keen was he to follow where Christ had gone.
On his way to Rome he took every opportunity of strengthening
and encouraging Christian congregations in the towns of Asia,
and he wrote several letters, one of them to Christians in Rome,
which expresses his state of mind in terms that speak for themselves:

> For my part, I am writing to all the churches and assuring them
> that I am truly earnest about dying for God—if only you yourselves
> put no obstacles in the way. I must implore you to do me no such
> untimely kindness; pray leave me to be a meal for the beasts, for
> it is they who can provide my way to God. I am his wheat, ground

> fine by the lion's teeth to be made purest bread for Christ. So intercede with him for me, that by their instrumentality I may be made a sacrifice for God.[1]

Stern words indeed! And of course, Ignatius was not typical of every early Christian. But Roman emperors seem to have had a passion for martyring bishops. Cyprian of Carthage (North Africa) met his end in 258. He had to wrestle with the problem of what to do with Christians who complied with the Roman authorities when they required everyone to sacrifice to the emperor. Ardent Christians refused to do this and risked the death penalty. Some Christians collaborated, hoping that persecution would end and they could go back to being Christians once more. As with the twentieth-century Church, Christians are often a mixed bag and include different degrees and types of commitment. But persecution, though sporadic in the ancient world (it did depend on where you lived, who the emperor was, and whether you were a Church official or not) and the phenomenon of martyrdom made the Church a strong group within society with a strong collective memory. It is no surprise at all that Christians in our century who face torture and possible death, either for being practicing Christians at all (behind the iron curtain) or for speaking out about racial conditions because of their Christian faith (in South Africa), look to those first Christians and their martyrs for exemplary faith, faith that kept them going through adverse conditions, faith that took them willingly to the end of their earthly lives.

(3)

What then of the evidence? So far we have mentioned circumstantial evidence, such as the plan of the church at Dura Europos and the letter of Ignatius of Antioch to the Church at Rome. There is other architectural evidence, and many other early Christian leaders wrote letters and they also preached sermons. Some of all of that has indeed come down to us. But there are certain important documents that we shall encounter repeatedly. They are either directly liturgical in their content or else they are descriptive, and because of the relative lack of material, they assume a relative importance.

First of all, the Bible provides us with evidence for all different sorts of worship, both Jewish and Christian. In the pages of the New Testament there are not only descriptions of services such as the baptism by Philip of the Ethiopian eunuch (see Acts 8:26ff.). We also come across the institution narratives of the Eucharist (see 1 Cor 11:23-26; Luke 22:15-20; Mark 14:22-25; Matt 26:26-29). Among other liturgical material, the possibility that some of the New Testament contains early Christian hymns and chants must not be overlooked (e.g., the *Magnificat*, see Luke 1:46-55).

Secondly, we have a document called the *Didache*, which means the "teaching." Long lost in antiquity, it was only rediscovered in 1873. Opinions differ as to where and when it was written, though there is a generally cautious agreement that it dates from the latter part of the first century and may have been written in Syria. It was written in Greek but was translated into at least one other language, Coptic, which means that it must have been used in Egypt. Its rediscovery caused as much astonishment in the Victorians as did the discovery of the Dead Sea Scrolls over forty years ago. Excitement was partly caused by the fact that scholars had known of its existence, as it is referred to by Christian writers three centuries later. This "Teaching of the Apostles" tells us how an early Christian community should work. It includes rules about baptism, fasting, and (it is generally agreed) about the Eucharist.

Thirdly, there are the writings of Justin Martyr. Justin was born in Syria and was converted to Christianity in 130 after trying some of the other religions offered in the ancient world. His most important work is the *First Apology*, written about 150. An "apology," so far from saying "sorry," is in fact a defense of the

Christian faith. Justin is trying to show that it is possible to be a practicing Christian and also be both an intelligent person and a loyal Roman citizen. In the *First Apology* are two important descriptions of the Eucharist. When we look at them, we must remember that unlike the author of the *Didache,* Justin is writing for outsiders so that his language is as void of esoteric Christian terminology as possible. That sort of care with words is another lesson for Christians today, who are often rightly accused of using their own language when attempting a dialogue with the world.

Fourthly, there is the *Apostolic Tradition* of Hippolytus. Like the *Didache,* this document is a Church order describing the discipline and arrangements for a Christian community. Also like the *Didache,* it was only identified recently, thanks largely to the work of scholars at the beginning of the twentieth century. As the title suggests, it purports to be truly apostolic, that is, coming straight from the hands of the apostles. We now know that it is the work (at least in editing) of Hippolytus, who was a presbyter (or priest) in Rome at the start of the third century, and the *Apostolic Tradition* has been dated to about 215. Much longer than the *Didache,* it contains detailed prescriptions about daily prayer, baptism, Eucharist, and ordination. It shows us a tightly knit and well-organized community. Although it may not be typical (we shall be looking at other documents of the same century to show some contrast), nevertheless, the *Apostolic Tradition* influenced other such Church orders in the ancient world, notably in the eastern Mediterranean. Originally written in Greek, the earliest text that we have is a fifth-century Latin translation.

All of this needs to be set against a background of which we see only glimpses. For example, in Rome alone there appear to have been around twenty thousand Christians in the middle of the third century out of a population of at least eighty thousand. And this community alone contained several different nationalities, as one would expect in that city at that time. Doubtless this meant regional churches in various parts of Rome worshiping in different languages, which would certainly include both Latin and Greek. Such a cautionary note, then, will help us use our main evidence creatively. Yes, there were procedures, but the procedures included variety both within the documents available to us and also in those which are not available. In the East the linguistic pattern must have been even more varied. When we look at the Eucharistic prayer we shall be able to see, even in English translation, the direct results of Semitic and Greek cultures coming through the Syriac and Greek prayers of the third century. All this was to meet the basic need, expressed eloquently in the vision of all the main peoples of the then-known world telling the wonders of God in their own tongues (see Acts 2:1-11).

2: Daily Prayer

(1)

Today's Church in its life of daily prayer does not stand up to favorable comparison with what we know of antiquity. It is true that there has been enormous revival of the Eucharist in the Western Churches. People are receiving Communion with more frequency than they have for centuries. But the cost has been considerable, particularly in two main areas.

First, what we might call *noneucharistic* worship has suffered in consequence. In many of the Churches where the Eucharist has regained its centrality, the infrastructure has all but disappeared. By ''infrastructure'' I mean forms of daily morning and evening prayer that have been recited at least on Sundays in most Churches for many years. For Anglicans, the obvious cases are the decline of Matins and evensong. Matins, in the *Book of Common Prayer* text, has no sermon and no blessing at the end; it tails off with a few collects. Why? Because the original drafters of the prayer book intended Matins to be followed by the Eucharist on every Sunday and major occasion in the Church year. Evensong, on the other hand, was intended to be a corresponding act of daily praise to sanctify the latter part of the day. Preaching, if any, was supposed to take place during the (weekly) Eucharist.

Now all of that has changed. Evensong, like evening services in other Churches, has either declined into a quiet, meditative service for a relatively small congregation, or else it has grown into a large, sometimes quite informal mission-type service. But before we speak further about mission-services, a few more words are required on this infrastructure theme.

When the Eucharist is *supported* by daily prayer, it is able to arise out of daily prayer, whatever form that might take. (As this chapter will show, the forms have varied considerably in length, style, and scope.) When, however, daily prayer declines into being something which the clergy do on their own, and the faithful rush into the Eucharist at the last minute without much preparation, then the Eucharist on a Sunday morning often has to carry a far greater load than it is meant to do. There are many Christian communities these days that only meet on Sunday mornings for a Eucharist that cannot last much more than an hour, and into those sixty minutes the whole of its life has to be celebrated and the preaching has to combine teaching, exegesis, moral exhortation, and devotion. No wonder that some churches are beginning to consider extending the Sunday service to make more of the opportunity of the gathered congregation.

The development of the mission-service, akin to the family service, has produced another gap in the diet of many Christians today, as they flock to more and more Eucharists. What is missing is the didactic form of service whose main ingredient is the reading and preaching of the Word. Early evidence suggests that our forebears knew of instruction liturgies. They certainly had to attend them if they were candidates for baptism. Perhaps here there is a continuum as much with the debating societies of the ancient world where ideas are explored and discussed as with the synagogue with its regular Sabbath worship (which we shall look at shortly).

Such services of instruction, whether today or in antiquity, are not meant just for new initiates to the faith or even enquirers. In any case, today's Churches are much more public and "open" than in the early centuries. Then, particularly in times of persecution, Church officials themselves took careful note of who attended services, and noncommunicants came to be excluded from attending the second part of the Eucharist. Liturgies of instruction are meant for the edification of the faithful as well as for the basic instruction of members who are relatively new to the Christian faith. Moreover, it needs to be said that not everyone is at the same stage of faith, and many of us need to hear the same thing said to us by a preacher or a teacher several times in different ways in our lives before the truth begins to sink in!

Modern Christians approach the phenomenon of daily prayer in the early Church with these two handicaps: an overfamiliarity with the Eucharist and a tendency to regard services of instruction as only intended for certain types of people (enquirers, newcomers, or at best, intense Christians such as evangelicals!). But they come with a third handicap which is yet more basic.

By the very structures of our society and church life, we tend to drive a wedge between "corporate" and "private" prayer. We speak of "corporate" prayer mainly in terms of what goes on in a church building, which is usually structured in some way, whether the form of service is taken from a centrally authorized book or whether it is based on some more local plan. Then, we speak of "private" prayer as something done silently on one's own or else by a very small group of people at home (which tends to be quite rare). That is the tacit assumption behind a lot of people's approach to prayer, and it is unwittingly encouraged by patterns of church worship all through the age range, compounded often by the pressure to teach small children childish types of prayer at bedtime, from which they never grow into something more mature and adult. Many are the people today who when under pressure of some grave accident or tragedy in adulthood suddenly regress into the very simple prayers taught them as children because they know no others.

Antiquity knew no such division. There was no such thing as "silent prayer": If one had a prayer, then it was recited aloud, even on one's own. And there was enough of a corporate focus in the life of the local Church to enable those who prayed on their own to feel part of the rest of the community as they prayed.

(2)

The early Church was born into a world very different from ours. Its inheritance in daily prayer was threefold. First, there was the Jewish Temple, destroyed in the year 70. In its elaborate cultic worship there were two sacrifices, morning and evening, which the priests took turns in offering. On Sabbaths, new moons, and feasts these were *three* in number and offered morning, afternoon, and evening. The priests who took turns spending two weeks at a time in Jerusalem to perform these functions were often accompanied by a group of people from the locality concerned. To express solidarity with the priests at the Temple, there would be a time of prayer in that locality when their priests were making the offering in the Temple, morning and evening.

Secondly, there was the synagogue. No one knows for certain *when* and *why* the synagogue developed. It was once thought that it grew up during the Exile because the Temple was not available, or else it was invented to cope with a growing nation for whom the Temple could not have the impact that it should except on an occasional basis. Remember that Joseph, Mary, and Jesus traveled to the Temple in Jerusalem all the way from Nazareth when Jesus was twelve, which must have been a very special occasion for all three of them, traveling as they did in what appears to be a local extended family group (see Luke 2:41ff.). We know, however, that synagogues had services every Sabbath; some synagogues also had services on Mondays and Thursdays, which were the market days; and it is possible that a few synagogues actually went the whole hog and had *daily* worship.

Thirdly, there was the tradition of the pious Jew, who was supposed to pray daily. *What* they were supposed to pray naturally related to both the Temple and the synagogue. There is some evidence to suggest that this took place three times a day (see Dan 6:10, 9:21 and Ps 55:17). Like the synagogue service, such prayer probably included blessing prayers (known as *berakah* prayers from the Hebrew opening word), which for the very de-

vout Jew were many in number and came to be applied to virtually every action in the course of a day. Such a spirituality is rooted
in the basic attitude of bringing the whole of the day into a conscious celebration of God's love. As for the synagogue service,
it may have included portions of the Psalter; it would certainly
have involved *berakah* prayers (such as the time-honored eight-
een blessings), as well as readings from the Law (prophets on
Sabbaths), sometimes with exposition.

Jewish background is important. As Gregory Dix, a renowned
scholar, said in a lecture forty years ago: "Our understanding
of our forms of worship underwent a radical transformation . . .
when it finally occurred to someone that Jesus was a Jew." And
that, indeed, was the religious background of Jesus. He attended
the Temple and the synagogue. On one notable occasion (see
Luke 4:16ff.) he went to his own local synagogue and was asked
to read from the Scriptures on a Sabbath. Having read Isa 61:1-2,
he gave the scroll which contained the prophets back to the at-
tendant and sat down in the chair of Moses to speak to the people.
At every step, save, of course, in what he said in his sermon,
he followed established procedure. As a visiting rabbi, perhaps,
he was accorded the privilege of carrying out the reading and
preaching the sermon.

When we look more closely at the New Testament, we find
that the threefold influence of Temple, synagogue, and domestic prayer permeates references to Jesus, the disciples, and early
Christians actually praying. We are told to pray without ceasing
(see Luke 21:36), and that Cornelius prayed constantly to God
(see Acts 10:2). As if that were not enough, we are exhorted to
persevere in prayer (see Rom 12:12), as did the first Christians
(see Acts 2:42). Jesus gives his disciples the Lord's Prayer (see
Matt 6:9-13), a prayer so familiar to Christians that we perhaps
forget that it was the last Jewish prayer composed before the dawn
of the Christian Church. Some chance references in the epistles
give us a clue as to what early Christian worship contained, such
as a hymn, an instruction, a revelation, a tongue (see 1 Cor 14:26).

The early Christians gathered in Mary's house for prayer (see Acts 12:12). But they also went to the Temple (see Luke 24:53), a practice that persisted until they were eventually excluded.

There are also indications that individuals or groups "sanctified" the various parts of the day (see Mark 13:35), and Jesus took opportunities to pray through the night (see Luke 6:12), something akin to Paul and Silas praying and singing at midnight (see Acts 16:25). The symbolism of light in darkness (see John 8:12; Luke 12:35) may not be unrelated to the practice of ritually lighting lamps at home on the eve of Sabbaths. It was that custom that was to give rise to the lighting of candles at Vespers (evening worship) in the early centuries, which continues to this day in the Orthodox Church and is being revived in many modern service books.

What does all this amount to? It shows us a picture of a group of people anxious to fulfill the commands of Jesus in their worship and living. It also shows us a great deal about the balance of corporate, group, and individual prayer that arose out of the New Testament. True, the structures of Church life were quite different then from what they are today, but we get no picture whatever of the kind of sharp division between prayer in a church building and ordinary lay spirituality. Rather, there is almost a sense of interplay between the two—that is, if it is possible at all to divide the Church of the New Testament into "lay" and "ordained," a division hard to justify at such an early stage.

We must not forget, too, that the New Testament contains certain liturgical hymns. We have already mentioned the *Magnificat* (Luke 1:46-55). There is also material such as the canticle of Phil 2:5-11, which may well have been an early Christian hymn.

(3)

When we leave the New Testament, our evidence takes on a different character. The *Didache* gives us the following important recommendation:

> Do not keep the same fast days as the hypocrites. Mondays and
> Thursdays are their days for fasting, so yours should be Wednes-
> days and Fridays.
>
> Your prayers, too, should be different from theirs. Pray as the
> Lord enjoined in his Gospel: Our Father . . . . Say this prayer
> three times every day.[2]

The didachist here gives us a great deal in a few words. The Jews
(who are "the hypocrites") fast on Mondays and Thursdays (the
market days when some synagogues, perhaps those in market-
towns, had services), so Christians must do so on Wednesdays
and Fridays. This tradition survives into later Christian history
and explains why, for example, when the Eucharist came to be
celebrated on weekdays as well as Sundays, in many places Wednesdays and Fridays were chosen as appropriate fast days. Secondly, the Lord's Prayer is to be the foundation of all Christian
prayer, and it should be recited three times a day. At what hours?
Most agree that this means morning, noon, and evening, the three
natural divisions of the day. In the middle of the third century
Cyprian hammered home the significance of the Lord's Prayer
as the model for all Christian prayer when he pointed out that
we do not pray "My Father" but "Our Father."

But there is still an insistence that prayer and life should be
at one, a fear perhaps that the new religion might repeat some
of the institutional habits of the old. Thus, to offset the recommendation of Clement of Rome (*ca.* 90) that "we should do in
order everything that the Lord commanded us to do at set times,"
the other Clement, of Alexandria (*ca.* 150–215), trumpets that "we
are bidden to worship . . . not on special days as some do, but
continuously all our life through, and in all possible ways." He
goes on: "All our life is a festival: being persuaded that God is
everywhere present on all sides, we praise him as we till the
ground, we sing hymns as we sail the sea, we feel his inspiration in all that we do."

Nonetheless, for all the fine-sounding words that worship and
life belong together, Christian communities need to be organized

and require some sort of routine. The *Apostolic Tradition* of Hippolytus gives us a lengthy series of directions on daily prayer, though the section concerned may come from a slightly later version of the text. It is a long passage, but some parts of it are worth quoting in full:

> Let every faithful man and woman, when they have risen from sleep in the morning, before they touch any work at all, wash their hands and pray to God, and so go to their work. But if instruction in the word of God is given, each one should choose to go to that place, reckoning in his heart that it is God whom he hears in the instructor. . . .
>
> If there is a day when there is no instruction, let each one, when he is at home, take up a holy book and read in it sufficiently what seems to him to bring profit.[3]

Here is a clear distinction between *prayer* on rising from bed and *instruction*, whether on special days in church or of a more private character.

> And if you are at home, pray at the third hour and bless God. . . . For at that hour Christ was nailed to the tree.
>
> Pray likewise at the time of the sixth hour. For when Christ was nailed to the wood of the cross, the day was divided, and darkness fell.
>
> And at the ninth hour let them pray also a great prayer and a great blessing. . . .
>
> Pray before your body rests on the bed. Rise about midnight, wash your hands with water and pray. If your wife is present also, pray both together; if she is not yet among the faithful, go apart into another room and pray; and go back to bed again. Do not be lazy about praying. He who is bound in the marriage bond is not defiled.
>
> And likewise rise about cockcrow, and pray. For at that hour, as the cock crew, the children of Israel denied Christ, whom we know by faith. . . .[4]

Here is clear evidence for set hours of prayer throughout the day.

> Always reverently observe to sign your forehead. For this sign of the passion is known and approved against the devil.[5]

It is difficult to tell what *form* these hours of prayer took. A picture emerges in the early centuries of using certain psalms associated with certain hours or days. Tertullian, who lived at Carthage (*ca.* 160–225), mentions that ''the more conscientious in prayer are accustomed to append to their prayers Alleluia and such manner of psalms, so that those who are present may respond with the endings of them.'' Eusebius of Caesarea (Palestine, *ca.* 260–340) is the first person to be explicit about formal daily prayer ''in church,'' as we would say:

> Throughout the world in the churches of God in the morning, at sunrise, and in the evening, praises and truly divine pleasures are constituted to God. . . .
>
> The practice of singing psalms in the name of the Lord is observed everywhere; for this commandment to sing psalmody is in force in all the churches existing among the peoples. . . .
>
> In the whole world, in towns and villages as well as in the fields, in a word, in all the Church, the peoples of Christ gathered in all the nations sing with a loud voice hymns and psalms to the only God. . . .[6]

In a book attributed to Eusebius we come across specific directions of twenty-four psalms to be said at each hour of the day and night. The morning psalms are 63, 141, and 142. The psalms for the evening are 113, 130, and 141; they are to accompany the lighting of the lamps. As with so much Christian worship, evidence becomes more firm and detailed from the fourth century onward, as the Church becomes more organized and prominent. But what of those first three centuries and what they say of daily prayer?

The texts quoted leave us in no doubt that the practice of regular times of prayer existed from the earliest years and they seem to indicate fairly short, rhythmical miniliturgies, easily memorable and quite different from the elaborate offices of later monasticism. It would be tempting to string the *Apostolic Tradition* of Hippolytus and the prescriptions of Eusebius together in order to form a complex whole. That would be to misuse the evidence.

But Hippolytus' directions have a more domestic flavor than do those of Eusebius. Whereas Hippolytus envisages a married couple praying simply at home and taking care to attend to religious instruction liturgies when these are available, Eusebius seems to have in mind a more complicated round of church services, in which all join in according to their ability. It is a fact of liturgical life that people do tend to describe services according to their own slant or viewpoint. Also, it needs to be borne in mind that Hippolytus may be reproducing a tradition, a Church order already established, whereas Eusebius is simply laying down his own law in lavish, idealistic measure.

Nevertheless, from the quotations given above and from other writers, we can depict the *ideal* of domestic prayer as the foundation of the Church's worship, centering around the recitation of certain select psalms together with prayers of blessing (perhaps adaptations of the Jewish *berakah* prayers) and the Lord's Prayer. We know that Christians prayed to the East, waiting for the Second Coming, in much the way portrayed by the illustration at the head of this chapter.

How often these prayers would be offered would, of course, vary according to circumstance. In many places there was a tendency to focus on three main parts of the day, whether by domestic prayer at home or else, if circumstances permitted it, in the place where the church met. These hours were morning, noon, and evening. In some regions, it seems, the morning hour was near dawn and the evening hour near sunset. In other places, including Rome (if Hippolytus is reliable), morning prayer was at the third hour whereas evening prayer took place at the ninth hour. The first pattern is based on the natural solar division of the day whereas the second is more symbolic in its reasoning, following as it does the passion narrative and/or the morning and evening sacrifices in the Temple.

But these are details. The main thrust of daily prayer in this formative era of the Christian Church is to state boldly that prayer belongs to *all* Christians, not just the clergy, and that, therefore, it is not something that the clergy should be doing "for" the laity. True, there was emerging a monastic movement that was far more rigorous and tough in its ideals and practices concerning daily prayer, and their successors are alive today in the thousands of religious communities all over the world, including such well-known places as Taizé. But these are really exceptions—or they *should* be. It is so easy for Christians to sell out the merely possible to the superlatives of the ideal, far more difficult to plod on with the manageable and ordinary. But that is our duty and service. So whether in sanctifying ordinary daily hours or in attending to simple instruction, we have a considerable heritage to cheer us on as we seek to pray daily in our own way.

3: Making New Christians

(1)

The sounds of a baby crying in a church are for many people a signal that there is a baptism going on. It rings bells with us about birth, about origins, about a special occasion in which family, friends, the rest of the congregation, take part. One of the most acute tensions within the Western Churches today concerns the way in which baptism is carried out both in pastoral policy and in what we may reasonably call liturgical style.

The baby crying may well be doing so at a hole-in-the-corner baptism on a Sunday afternoon, the congregation exclusively family and friends. The local pastor has perhaps been pressured into presiding at such a service by influential people who may only come to church once a year, if that. There is an impressive array of Sunday hats. The baby may even be late for its own baptism because the limousine couldn't get there on time. Pastor and church doorkeeper stand at the entrance to the church, silently seething as yet one more exercise in consumer religion seems to be about to take place. The photo session after the service is lengthy. The pastor has already had a grueling Sunday morning, in the course of which he has preached three times in three different places. All he wants to do is go home, put his feet up, and rest—before his fourth sermon, at evensong.

Such a caricature may not be entirely fair to both sides. The family may have very good reasons for a supposed "private" bap-

31

tism (for that is what it is, to all intents and purposes). And it is very difficult for "fringe" folk who have for generations learned that baptism *is* something private, on a Sunday afternoon suddenly to digest the fine rhetoric of the twentieth-century Church that speaks of participation, a corporate focus, ancient traditions, and that least desirable thing of all, involvement in the local community.

There are other forces at work too. The Western Churches still tend to be blurred at the edges of church membership, which results in larger congregations at festivals than on ordinary Sundays. Moreover, baptism, which was so highly valued by the earliest Christians, is for many people at the edge of membership something they feel needs to be *done*, this by instinct rather than because of articulated theological conviction.

If you look at the new service books of the mainstream Churches today, you will find two somewhat different routes toward membership in the Church. One is a revision of what most people regard as the traditional method but which, as we shall see, is anything but ancient. This scheme has infant baptism, followed at some later stage by a rite called confirmation or perhaps admission to full membership. The difference now lies in the fact that both these services are recommended to take place during the main Sunday service of the local congregation. And that's where the tension often comes to a head, because many families do not easily identify with the Sunday congregation and they will make every excuse to have the service in the way that it developed in the Middle Ages, the way described in caricature at the beginning of this chapter.

To compound the difficulty, these service books set before us another model, one which places baptism and confirmation together within a corporate rite intended for those able to answer for themselves. *The Book of Common Prayer* of 1662 does have a form of baptism for those of riper years (as they are delicately described!). Now that provision has caught up with us in a big way. And this second model, as we shall see, is far closer to what the first Christians knew but with the subtle difference that they did not divide people up quite so neatly into age groups. The fact is that this second method of Christian initiation is being used all over the Western world by Roman Catholics, Anglicans, Lutherans, Methodists, Presbyterians, and Congregationalists. With the gradual breakup of Christendom and the decline in the number of infant baptisms, it is inevitable that a missionary Church is going to encounter the results of that decline. Every year since I was ordained I have come across people who want to be confirmed at the annual confirmation but who are shy or diffident about it because they aren't baptized. What has often ensued is a deeply impressive confirmation Eucharist, at which those people are baptized by the bishop himself, thus eloquently stating to all and sundry that baptism, not confirmation, is the primal sacrament of Christian membership.

Today we have inherited both these norms from the past. The infant baptism-plus-later-confirmation pattern arose in the Middle Ages and survived the Reformation. In terms of pastoral practice, the Reformation really made little difference, even though the rites concerned were considerably simplified for Anglicans, Lutherans, Methodists, Presbyterians, and Congregationalists. The other pattern which is gaining ground so fast now is based on the much earlier procedures of the Church as they emerged from the New Testament and the first Christian centuries.

What might these norms say to the hole-in-the-corner syndrome that we have also inherited? Different Churches are going to respond in different ways, according to their own contexts. It may well be more accommodating in a village but more demanding on a housing estate. On the other hand, it would be a pity if neither side were able to look critically at what the inheritance is and then find out a way of appraising it and asking everyone, starting with the local congregation, how to move forward practically in a way that matches up to the demands of the gospel. Once again, we all need to be challenged. But one word of caution. It is very easy for enthusiastic Christians to hit others with a new fad. Geoffrey Lampe wrote tellingly of tests of church membership a few years ago:

> The most searching test . . . is probably that which the Christian community, represented by the local congregation, ought to apply to itself: can it undertake to care for new members, children especially, in such a way as to communicate the Christ-Spirit to them, and is it a recognizably Spirit-inspired body? Is it, in other words, worth joining?[7]

(2)

Why be baptized? The New Testament gives us part of the answer. Jesus himself went down into the water and was baptized by John (see Mark 1:9-11; Matt 3:13-17; Luke 3:21-2; John 1:29-34). It was different from other baptisms performed by John because, as we read, Jesus' baptism gave him a new sense of identity. He was washed—and the Spirit came upon him, calling him God's Son.

Ritual baths were a common feature in the ancient world. It is possible that the Jews practiced some sort of ritual washing of converts from outside their race (proselytes). We know that the famous Dead Sea communities had ritual baths repeatedly. But Christian baptism connotes so many different aspects of the gospel that it has to stand out from any possible antecedents that it may have had. Paul speaks of baptism as dying and rising with Christ (see Rom 6:3-11), the logic of which is to suggest that the reason for being baptized is not that Jesus himself was baptized but rather because he rose from the dead. He also speaks of us having "put on" Christ as a garment, which may well be an allusion to baptism itself (see Gal 3:27). At the end of the First Gospel, Jesus commands his followers to convert the world and baptize everyone (see Matt 28:19). It is not a coincidence that he connects preaching, conversion, and baptism and that baptism must be in the name of the Trinity, perhaps as a safeguard against using other names or formulas.

One of the first accounts of baptism we have is in the Acts of the Apostles (see 8:26ff.). It's a remarkable story about the missionary Church—Philip the deacon going south and meeting a potential convert who is reading what we would call his Old Testament. In the story, however, are the seeds of what became the standard procedure in the liturgies that began to grow up all over the Christian world in those early centuries. The convert first of all expresses interest—and has the Scriptures explained to him on a journey which might last some time. That becomes the profession of faith, backed up by a series of instructions beforehand. Then both minister and convert go down into the water and the baptism takes place, probably using water quite lavishly. The minister, Philip, identifies himself with what is going on by being there in the water.

The early centuries added lots of things to this bare procedure. One of the first was a rich approach to symbolism, starting with the *water*. It meant washing—for the forgiveness of sins. It meant the pouring out of the Spirit—like the water being poured over the head of the new Christian. It also meant taking part in a symbolic way in Jesus' death and burial. As with a great Christian mystery, it is hard to hold everything together even within an elaborate liturgy—though there is no question yet of great elaboration. But the evidence for procedure and collective discipline is early and impressive. The *Didache* is specific:

> The procedure for baptizing is as follows. After repeating all that has been said [i.e., the precepts regarding the ways of life and death, in the previous chapters], immerse in running water "In the name of the Father, and of the Son, and of the Holy Ghost." If no running water is available, immerse in ordinary water. This should be cold if possible, otherwise warm. If neither is practicable, then pour water three times on the head. . . . Both baptizer and baptized ought to fast before the baptism, as well as any others who can do so; but the candidate himself should be told to keep a fast for a day or two beforehand.[8]

Some of this reads a little like a cookbook! But it tells us nonetheless the detailed care which the earliest Christian writers were prepared to take in writing of this sacred moment. In a climate where water is not always easily available, it seems that a tub or a stream fit best into the ideal. The threefold name must be used. There must be preparation, which includes fasting as well as instruction. A similar pattern emerges from Justin Martyr's *First Apology,* though there is more explanation of the meaning of the washing along biblical lines. One can imagine a baptism such as this taking place in the baptistery in the church at Dura Europos. The font is large enough for an adult to kneel down in and have water poured from a large pitcher—thus keeping the tradition of having fresh and living water as the instrument of baptism.

A fuller account of a baptism is to be found in the *Apocryphal Acts of Judas Thomas,* which was written in Syria at the beginning of the third century. It is supposed to give accounts of the missionary wanderings of the apostle, but it's much more likely to reflect how the Syrian Church in the late second and early third centuries carried out baptism. It may well reflect even earlier practice. After all, a persecuted Church is not one that is likely to change its liturgies all the time. Here is the story of the baptism of King Gundaphorus:

> And the king gave orders that the bath should be closed for seven days, and that no man should bathe in it. And when the seven days were done, on the eighth day the three entered into the bath by night. . . . And many lamps were lighted in the bath.
>
> And when they had entered into the bath-house, Judas went in before them. And our Lord appeared unto them, and said, "Peace be with you, my brethren." And they heard the voice only, but the form they did not see, whose it was, for till now they had not been baptized. And Judas went up and stood upon the edge of the cistern, and poured oil upon their heads, and said: "Come, holy name of the Messiah; come, power of grace . . . come Spirit of holiness, and purify their reins and their hearts." And he baptized them in the Name of the Father and of the Son and of the

Spirit of holiness. And when they had come up out of the water, a youth appeared to them, and he was holding a lighted taper; and the light of the lamps became pale through its light. . . . And when it dawned and was morning, he broke the Eucharist.[9]

If we read between the lines we glimpse a definite series of procedures. The baths have to be prepared seven days beforehand—some Christians fasted before baptism (as we have seen) as *their* preparation. The apostle doesn't go into the water but stands on the edge of the cistern—a sizeable pool. And before the actual baptism, he pours *oil* over the heads of the candidates and recites a prayer of invocation for them and then baptizes them in the name of the Trinity. The room where the baptisms are celebrated appears to be *lit* with special lamps, and when the baptisms have been completed, a special lamp is carried in. Finally, the service leads straight into a dawn Eucharist, the clear implication being that the three new Christians receive Communion with everyone else.

So there are a number of new features here. A time of preparation corresponds with what we have seen already. But pouring oil? It is not quite so strange as it seems, even in today's world, in which oil has two main uses—keeping engines going and cooking fatty meals! Oil is still used when the British sovereign is crowned in Westminster Abbey. It is mentioned in many contexts in the Bible, not just at coronations of monarchs but at ordinations of priests and prophets in the Old Testament, as well as for healing the sick (see Jas 5:13ff.) and embalming (see Luke 23:56) in the New. The anointing of the Holy Spirit (see 2 Cor 1:21f.) is also an expression found in the New Testament. At some stage, we do not know exactly when, oil entered the baptismal liturgy and it came to be used in different ways. In time, it was used *twice*—once over the whole body before baptism in the same way that we use soap when we are washing, and then just on the head as a perfume when the bath was over. It's clear, however, that the single use of oil in the baptism of Gundaphorus just described is a symbol of the descent of the Spirit.

The other symbolism is that of light which is brought into the baptismal chamber. In time, this becomes a candle that was given to the newly baptized when they moved from the baptistery into church. Everyone else would have had a candle or lamp, as the service began late at night and ended early in the morning. What started life as a necessity (being able to see in the dark) eventually became a symbol (possessing the light of Christ). Practicalities determined how things were done. Because of modesty, candidates for baptism who were women were cared for at the font by deaconesses. As one third-century Christian manual puts it, "it is not fitting that women should be seen by men"— especially if you belong to an organization which is being criticized for its teachings about love, unity, and equality.

As local churches became more structured, so too did that period before baptism. Toward the end of the second century, we begin to read of people called "catechumens." The word comes from the Greek word "to teach," though it originally had a cruder meaning, "to din in"! A catechumen is someone who is being taught about the Christian faith, and it is from that word that we get "catechism," the body of Christian teaching which came to be very popular in the later Middle Ages and after.

Catechumens had certain rights. They were expected to make offerings like anyone else and take part in the life of the local Christian congregation. But they were not allowed to receive Communion since they were not yet baptized. So important was this rule that the catechumens were actually sent out of church after the first part of the Eucharist, just before the sharing of the peace and the preparation of the altar table. Not to be present during that second part of the service must have had a considerable impact upon them. Deliberate and sometimes lengthy exclusions from certain things would have affected catechumens and communicants alike. One wonders what sort of "exodus" must have resulted in some congregations.

How long did the catechumenate last? This is a little like asking how long is a piece of string. In some places it lasted as little as a few months, in other places it lasted three years. So awesomely was baptism regarded that some people started to recommend *delaying* it, as Tertullian himself did at Carthage toward the end of the second century. And that, of course, brought with it the debate about whether or not children should be baptized. Since baptism and access to Communion were in those days inseparable, not to baptize children meant excluding them from the Eucharist also. Tertullian also gives us evidence for another trend, which was to confine celebrations of baptism to major festivals, in those days Easter and Pentecost (Christmas had not yet gotten into the calendar).

Much of all this comes together in the *Apostolic Tradition* of Hippolytus. In a lengthy passage concerning baptism, he stipulates that the catechumenate should last three years. All along the line the whole congregation is involved in some way, instructing the new Christians, praying for them regularly (no doubt by name), and being present at the baptism itself which is supposed to take place overnight, between Saturday and Sunday. The finger points at the candidates themselves. *They* have to make the Christian profession of faith before being immersed in the water. That profession of faith becomes the basis of the later creeds. And the children are catered to, too. If they are not old enough to answer for themselves, they must have sponsors from their families. Moreover, *they* are baptized first of all, followed by the men, and the women last. There are two anointings now, before and after baptism, and the bishop, who presides over the entire service, lays his hand on the newly baptized just before the second anointing.

Liturgy is a curiously conservative business, for here in that hand laying by the presiding bishop, are the germs of what in the later West came to be called confirmation. Although this takes us beyond the early Church, it is worth recounting the bare details of the story. As Christianity spread through the west of Europe, the areas over which bishops presided (dioceses) became larger and larger, with the result that the local bishop could not be present at every service of baptism. So the little part of the rite which concerned laying his hand upon the candidates became separated from the rest of the service and was performed as the giving of the Spirit when he could get around to the local churches of his diocese. At the Reformation, Anglicans and some others kept confirmation but made the stipulation that it must be given only when people are old enough to understand. It thus also became a rite of conscious commitment to Christ. That may or may not be a fine development in itself, but it takes us yet further from the spirit of the early Church.

(3)

It is not really surprising that writer after writer in those far-off centuries links baptism with Easter. There is an old prayer that even calls baptism and Eucharist ''the Easter sacraments.'' Beneath all the differences of custom and the conflicting views about the most suitable age for baptism to be given, there lay the deep-down conviction that to be part of Christ meant sharing his risen life.

When set alongside what happens in many churches today, I think we must conclude that the early Christians valued baptism much more than we do. They would not understand that Sunday afternoon family gathering round a neat little font decorated with seasonal flowers. They *would*, however, approve of the growing tendency to put baptism back into the main act of worship. That is where many of the Reformers really wanted it, too. They would say that this is where it properly belongs. They would also ask us why we do not admit young children to Communion immediately after baptism. They would be utterly confused by confirmation.

From the evidence surveyed so far, it will be clear that the amount of water at baptism varied from place to place. But there is the underlying conviction that as much water as possible should be used in order to speak of the God who freely gives us his grace, forgiveness, and the power of his renewing love. Archaeological evidence such as the baptistery at Dura Europos conveys the special meaning attached to baptism and the dramatic effect it must have had not only on the initiates but on the whole community. Both essentially private and essentially public, the summation of many weeks of hard thought and preparation by the whole congregation, baptism Sundays must have been special, to say the least. In time those fonts were to grow even larger, so that in the centuries immediately following the Peace of Constantine (313), it was normal for a font to be large enough for an adult to stand in with the water coming up to the knee. However, it will also be clear that the type of baptism increasingly popular in certain circles today which is commonly called "immersion" will have been the exception rather than the rule in the lifetime of the New Testament and in those earliest Christian centuries.

There are, in conclusion, two further messages from the early Church to us. One is to help us to enjoy symbolism far more than we do at the moment. It was a bold and vigorous age that introduced anointings. Modern services are frequently marred by being wordy to the point of dullness. Secondly, we are so inherently individualistic that we need to learn again what it is to see baptism not as something that the Church "does to someone" but rather as a way of life in which we are all constantly growing.

4: At the Lord's Table: The Word

(1)

I remember attending a service in a Presbyterian church one Sunday morning. A fairly large congregation had gathered for the occasion and the service proceeded in what was (for them) the normal manner. We had a call to worship at the beginning, which led into a hymn. Then there were prayers of penitence. Readings followed, interspersed with hymns. The long prayer (of intercession) came next. Then came (after another hymn) a twenty-minute sermon, clearly regarded by the whole assembly (except those younger members who had other matters on their mind) as the most important part of the service. During the final hymn, the offering was received and the service seemed to end with the blessing.

Here was the result of the Reformation—and it struck me as strange because all the Reformation rhetoric was about getting people to participate, about taking the Mass away from the priest, and all that seemed to have happened was that the people came together for a service of the Word that was entirely dominated by their *minister* instead of a Mass dominated by their *priest*.

But the strangest thing of all was that after the service was over about a quarter of us (no more) moved forward to the front pews, and having said goodbye to the rest of the congregation at the door, the minister then reappeared with his elders, carrying bread and wine, and proceeded with a shortened celebration of communion. It was tacked on to the end of the main service. It was no more than an optional extra. Once again, it would seem, the Reformation hadn't yet done its proper job. Communion had *not* been restored to ordinary men and women as the staple diet of Christian people. In liturgical practice, therefore, quite a different message was being heard.

And I doubt whether a drastic change in that procedure would have gone down particularly well with that rural flock, still less any attempts to introduce a more participatory form of service. (Cries of "no popery" would soon have gone up—or else some anti-Anglican sentiment would have been expressed loud and clear.) It was to me in my naive way sad that the legacy of history had produced that pattern of worship and that the great sixteenth-century rebellion against Roman authority and conservative liturgical custom had not engendered a more radical and more deeply traditional form of service.

And herein lies the difficulty. In order to reform an order of service that has been inherited over the years you have to understand its own roots and also the basic principles of what you are trying to do. The Reformers in the Presbyterian Churches *thought* they were following the ideals of the primitive Church in many of the things they purported to do about Church government. We shall be looking at some of this in a later chapter. Over worship, and indeed over many other matters, they simply did not have sufficient knowledge about the early Church because the material was not available to them. Some of the more extreme Reformers who soon became Baptists came to hold baptism by immersion as the only scriptural way of being baptized. Yet, as we saw in the last chapter, there is ample evidence to suppose that, in the lifetime of the New Testament and soon after, no such regulations existed.

Over the past hundred years, our knowledge of the roots of Christian worship has grown enormously and we are able to piece together much more of what those early Christians might have done than previous generations of scholars were able to do. Some of the results of this advance in knowledge have been new service books. Moreover, much of this work has been done in common with other Christians, so that you can attend a service in a Roman Catholic, Anglican, Lutheran, Methodist, or United Reformed Church and see far greater similarities than you would ever have done fifty years ago. This holds good for ordinary Sunday services as well as those special occasions such as baptisms, ordinations, marriages, and funerals. Many of the old divisions that kept us so apart from each other have come to be understood as differences of *emphasis* rather than *substance*.

But the old differences are still around, under the surface, in the folk memory. We are still coming to terms with them. And that is why it is important to continue to look at our liturgical origins critically and to ask if we are being as faithful to the gospel as we should be. For example, the service in that Reformed Church with the "stay-behind" communion has been typical of much Protestant worship in recent centuries. It stems from what we might call a misleading conception of what those origins are. The service is divided into two parts. The first is a liturgy of the Word, attended by the whole congregation. The second is a liturgy of the sacrament, attended by a small proportion of it. But the division is clear. Word, with chants and prayers, is followed by sacrament, with no chants. (In some respects, it was the absence of *music* at the second part that made it feel so second class, particularly from within a tradition where sacred song is so powerful. Liturgical "backdrop" is an important element!)

The Reformers half understood what they were doing in allowing that way of doing the Eucharist to creep in, and they backed it up, no doubt, by the strictness with which some of them permitted only certain people to communicate. What we shall see in this chapter is that the Word and the sacrament, while being separate parts of the Eucharist, are inseparable from each other and form the basis of the normal Sunday service for every Christian. (The service described earlier was a "stay-behind" that was only available on certain Sundays—on normal Sundays no Eucharist was available at all.) When looking at the evidence, a very different picture will emerge.

(2)

The first Christians gathered for the Eucharist in much the same way as the Jews did for Passover. They met for a meal but first heard the story of liberation of their people from slavery in Egypt. They then shared (as they still do) special prepared food with bread and wine, and it was all accompanied by special prayers and blessings. Their *story* was recounted in the course of the meal. (Since Christians are the offspring of this tradition, it is only courteous that we understand it better than we do.)

The essential difference, however, is that when Jesus shared the Last Supper with the disciples, he told them to "do this in remembrance of me." *He* was to be at the heart of the new fellowship, and it should be repeated often and not be something done only once a year. The New Testament gives us a lot of material on the Eucharist, but perhaps the most telling of all comes at the end of Luke's Gospel (see Luke 24:13-32), the story of the walk to Emmaus. In this story are contained the seeds of every Christian Eucharist, whatever the denomination or label. The two disciples walk on the road; the "way" is an early Christian codeword for the new religion. They are intent upon the Scriptures, but they can only understand them if they receive an explanation, and only Christ can give that. The mysterious stranger comes upon the scene to fulfill that function. There is a devotional intensity about what is going on, and as the walk ends, Jesus, elusive as ever, starts going away, but they ask him to stay behind and break bread with them. At the point when he breaks the bread (a traditional practice for Jews at home), they recognize him at last.

The two parts of the story, the walk with the Scriptures and the meal at table, correspond to the two essential ingredients of every Eucharist, as we have already seen in the Reformed service described earlier. They have indeed been clarified in today's new rites. You could spot them whether you go into a Baptist chapel, a Catholic cathedral, a Greek monastery, or a Methodist preaching hall, though with some of them you would have to look carefully. The first part is focused on the reading of Scriptures with a sermon and prayers. The second part leads to the preparation of the table, the thanksgiving, and the sharing of the bread and wine. Part one may, for dramatic reasons, center around a lectern or reading desk. Part two inevitably takes place at the table, the altar.

These two parts reflect the way Christians shared in the service by stages. In the previous chapter, we discussed how those who were preparing for baptism, the cathecumens, did not remain for the Communion but only stayed for the first part. Such a restriction would have reinforced the division of the liturgy into two parts, particularly in a fast-growing community with several or even many catechumens. That in turn became a mass exit of noncommunicants in later centuries, leading to the general reluctance of people to receive Communion more than a very few times in the year. This is a situation that has only recently begun to change.

When we move outside the New Testament, the evidence for that first part of the Eucharist is scanty but strong. In the *First Apology* of Justin Martyr we read the following account:

> And . . . we continually remind one another of these things. Those who have the means help all those in need; and we are always together.
>
> And we bless the Maker of all things through his Son Jesus Christ and through the Holy Spirit over all that we receive.
>
> And on the day called Sun-day an assembly is held in one place of all who live in town or country, and the records of all the apostles or writings of the prophets are read for as long as time allows.
>
> Then, when the reading has finished the president in a discourse admonishes and exhorts us to imitate these good things.
>
> Then we all stand up together and offer prayers.[10]

His account reveals several things, even if they only reflect what he knew of Roman practice in 150. (The fact that he speaks of "town or country" and writes with a universal scope suggests that he *is* describing fairly widespread liturgical practice in the Roman world.)

First of all, Christians gather at a local center every Sunday, which was then a normal working day. Then portions of what we would call the New Testament are read, with the amusing little direction, "for as long as time allows." That perhaps indicates the circumstances and social setting of their worship as much as any desire to read as much of the Scriptures as possible. The president (the term Justin uses for the person who "stands over" or "leads" public worship) preaches what we would call a sermon, the nature of which is to link the people of that community with the readings just read. The discourse isn't—or shouldn't be—a vague waffle. It has a purpose. The fact that Justin gives the sermon to the president, the presider, means that by at least the middle of the second century there is a sense of order within the community.

Because the sermon is based on the Scripture readings and sets out to apply the Christian faith to the people who are listening (or not!), the next step is to pray. This is done with everyone standing up, the traditional posture for prayer and one that is being revived today. That leads into the Eucharistic liturgy, the service of the sacrament, which we shall look at in the next chapter.

Scholars have thought for some time that this simple service of the Word is based, consciously or not, on the synagogue liturgy with which many of the early Christians would have been familiar. It would explain, perhaps, why the Christians began by attending synagogue and only when they were excluded did they have to produce their own Word service. More important, it would explain the close similarities of structure between the two liturgies, based on readings from Scripture, followed by a sermon, followed by prayer. There is an internal logic to this pattern of things. No one would ever think of starting with the sermon and ending up with the readings. To do things in decent order enables the community to have a sense of stability and purpose.

Another feature of this Jewish heritage survives today in many of the churches that have bishops. If you go to a service where a bishop is taking a prominent part, you will see that he always has to sit in a special chair—and he'll even have a throne in his cathedral. (All a "cathedral" means is where his chair, *cathedra*, is situated, meaning where he is supposed to operate from.)

The early Christians appear to have *sat* their preachers in a chair, what in the synagogues is still to this day called "the chair of Moses," where Jesus preached from when he visited the synagogue in Nazareth (see Luke 4:16ff.). Such a teacher's chair made good sense as long as the building was not too large. Early Christian places of worship were, by our standards, comparatively small, so there was no problem about visibility and audibility until the fourth century, when the preaching desk, or ambo (later called the "pulpit"), was invented. Although we find it hard today to get used to the idea of the preacher *sitting down* (except for reasons of physical health), it was the natural consequence of Jewish precedent and academic custom in the ancient world. There are several very old churches which have the bishop's chair in the original position beyond the east end: Norwich and Canterbury cathedrals, for example. Although we cannot be absolutely certain about the layout of the interior in the church at Dura Europos, it is more than likely that the presidential chair was at the far end, unless it was somewhere in the body of the church. But chair there would have been, and from a chair the president would have led the first part of the Eucharist and services of daily prayer and instruction, and he would have preached sitting in that chair.

Because this was long before the invention of printing, the Scriptures were treated with great care and reverence. Local communities would have had their own copies of parts of the Old and New Testaments, the versions often differing slightly. Because having the Bible in scroll form was a bit unwieldy, the practice grew of writing lectionaries, which contained only those parts of the Bible that were actually read at services.

How did you select what to read? Nowadays people have their own favorite passages, because everyone can read and the Bible is easily available. But even given the choice that is before us, most people are affected by the parts of the Bible they hear read in church, and for the majority of Christians today that means those readings that are heard at special points in the Church year.

But the Church's year took a long time to emerge and to be agreed upon. Easter and Pentecost were the two earliest feasts of Christianity. Christmas was a long time in coming—it does not appear until the fourth century, and its commercialization dates from a far more recent time. But once you add times of preparation before the festivals and the increasingly famous martyr's birthdays as well as the courses of sermons given to catechumens during the Lent prior to their Easter baptism, you already have the foundations for a Church year, and the elaborate scheme of lectionaries that appear over the Christian world from the fourth century onward. The Church didn't trust the clergy just to pick their favorite passages. A corporate organization expects collective discipline—and many of us know how repetitive sermons can become when the same texts and themes keep occurring because that's the way the preacher has chosen them.

Sermons could be rich in rhetorical style, like this passage, which comes from the Easter sermon of Melito, who was Bishop of Sardis in Asia Minor about 170:

> He came on earth from heaven for suffering man, becoming incarnate in a virgin's womb from which he came forth as man; he took on himself the suffering man through a body capable of suffering, and put an end to the sufferings of the flesh, and through his spirit incapable of death he became the death of death which is destructive of man.

> For led like a lamb, and slaughtered like a sheep, he ransomed us from the slavery of the world of Egypt, and loosed us from the slavery of the devil as from the hand of Pharaoh, and sealed our souls with his own spirit, and our bodily members with his own blood.
>
> This is the one who covered death with a garment of reproach, who put the devil in mourning garb as Moses did Pharaoh. This is he who smote lawlessness and rendered injustice bereft of children as Moses did Egypt.[11]

One feature which stands out in many early sermons that have come down to us is the preoccupation our forebears had with their Jewish origins. The Old Testament was regularly read at Sunday worship, especially the Eucharist, until well into the fifth century when it started to drop out, perhaps because people were uninterested or else did not understand its significance. The Old Testament has returned to the Eucharist with the advent of new service books in all the Churches of the West today.

Many ancient sermons actually end with the call to pray. (In those days, the creed was only used at baptism, in an interrogatory form, so that it never interrupted the sequence of readings-sermon-intercessions.) These prayers of intercession often followed certain conventions. In the New Testament there is an important passage that urges the faithful to pray for the leaders of the nations and for the Church within them (see 1 Tim 2:1-2), making it clear that the Church is not supposed to live a ghetto life, unconcerned with what goes on in the world outside, but rather as a leaven in the lump of the people Christ comes to save. It is interesting that Christians from the very start had to live with that conflict, that tension, which recurs through the ages and is very much a factor Western Christians have to face today in a different form.

In the Roman Catholic Church, there are extended forms of intercession on Good Friday which employ texts that may well go right back to the third century. Each bidding for prayer is short, specific, and ends with an "aim," as if it were impossible to men-tion certain people or situations without wishing them well in the Lord. Here is one of them:

> Let us pray, dear friends,
> for the whole Church of God throughout the world,
> that God the almighty Father
> guide it and gather it together
> so that we may worship him
> in peace and tranquility.[12]

Each prayer probably ended with some sort of congregational response so that the community could show its approval. The simplicity and directness of these texts may explain why they have influenced modern styles of prayer writing. But much more important than *what* they say is *why* they say it—to pray for other people is one of the greatest privileges of the Christian life. That's why early Christians stood up to pray for Church and world the moment the sermon at Sunday Eucharist was over.

(3)

The relationship between Christians and Jews has always involved tensions of one sort or another. The continuity between them is something that modern Christians perhaps are more conscious of than Christians of any other time in history, except that very early period when the majority of Christians had been brought up as Jews but had been converted to the new faith. But the influence of the Jewish tradition lingered on, particularly in the old Syrian Church, some of whose congregations still worship in Aramaic to this day. In the illustration heading this chapter is one of those old Syrian churches, with the altar at the east end. But in the center of the building a podium is a Christian adaptation of the arrangements that can still be seen in synagogues all over the world. The ''ark'' of the covenant becomes the place where the Bible is kept and it has candles surrounding it instead of the Jewish *menorah* (seven-branched candlestick). Two lecterns are used, one for Gospel readings, the other for all other lections (the synagogue will only have had *one* reading desk). At the west end of this stage, or bema, are the seats for the bishop and clergy, very much among the people.

This architectural arrangement makes the right symbolic overtones. The Liturgy of the Word is essentially a "human-ward" part of worship and therefore rightly belongs among the people. The second part, that of the Eucharist, which we shall look at in the next chapter, is "God-ward" in its focus. For Christians expecting the Second Coming in a precarious world, to celebrate the Eucharist with everyone facing east, "until he comes," was the most natural posture to adopt.

All of this is far from our own world—or is it? Perhaps many modern services give the impression that all is well, that the community has everything well sewn up, that it doesn't really need the Lord. In our very different circumstances, perhaps it is confusing to try to emphasize one element of the Eucharist at the expense of the other. History, both Catholic and Protestant, is full of horrific lessons of exaggeration. God perhaps belongs in the balance!

5: At The Lord's Table: The Meal

(1)

"We're utterly obsessed with the Eucharist as the solution to all our problems," said an American professor recently. One can understand what he was getting at. Although there are still some Western Churches that have yet to hear of the liturgical movement with its emphasis on corporate worship, weekly Eucharists, biblical preaching, and a deep understanding of what worship is trying to say, in some respects one could maintain that the pendulum has swung in the opposite direction. Sometimes I hear bishops complaining that all they ever seem to do is celebrate the Eucharist, often in somewhat top-heavy celebrations in the course of which all sorts of special events are situated. Has the liturgically renewed Church forgotten how to worship at any other service?

We touched on this in an earlier chapter when looking at how the first Christians prayed daily and how valuable they found the practice of regular times of prayer. We also saw how there were services of instruction which were more didactic in their style. Many are the modern Christians who yearn for more teaching, and many clergy respond to this in a patronizing manner, as if it were beneath them to give the laity some basic information. (Information, it would seem, is in some circles an outmoded method of education!)

Insofar as the issue affects the Western Churches that have restyled their worship toward the Eucharist, it seems that history has played yet one more of its tricks on us. Once you solve certain problems you are bound to create others, and these need sifting and assessing. For example, I know a parish church where the acoustics are second to none in the area. That makes choral and instrumental music a joy and delight to listen to and to take part in. The final hymn of the morning Eucharist is one of the most thrilling moments, with the organ playing brightly, the choir processing down the center aisle, the congregation losing inhibitions and enjoying itself. That is one side of the coin. But the other side is what the church is like sometimes before the service starts. Being a friendly sort of community, newcomers are welcomed at the back of church. Because there are a number of families with young children, there is a lot of noise as folk come in. The choir has a practice beforehand in their vestry—also near the back of the church. When the congregation is particularly large, it is often difficult to blow the whistle on the noise and have some quiet.

We don't know what problems akin to these the early Christians encountered, though from chance references we do know that people treated sermons rather more informally than we do today. (John Chrysostom, who lived toward the end of the fourth century, used to be greeted with applause at the end of his preaching!) But we do know that they valued the Eucharist, to the extent that they did not slip into the Lord's Supper as if they were dropping in for tea. Perhaps the developments of the fourth century, which are outside the scope of this book, paint a rather more severe picture than many of us would be comfortable with; people delayed baptism or communicated increasingly infrequently— almost as if to protest that they were not worthy. Religious psychology is a strange business.

Another problem that is arising as a result of liturgical changes is what to do with the second part of the Eucharist. As we saw in the previous chapter, the *first* part of the service has a relatively simple structure, and many experiments today depart little from how that first part is framed in the new service books. Introductory prayers are often responsorial. There may be different types of music offered. And the sermon can be a simple, direct, storytelling affair, aimed primarily at the children. Intercession may take the form of a group of people praying for various topics that have arisen in the course of the preceding week.

But the *second* part sometimes feels as if the service books were once again being slavishly followed, really because there is little scope for simplifying or for involving the congregation more: for example, in the Eucharistic prayer. Some people, of course, welcome the set character of the service book, which is as set in the Roman Missal as it is in the books of the other Churches. One of the reasons, perhaps, for this spiritual hunger is that we need to learn what it is to *pray the liturgy*, rather than to *read* or *say* it. If the average Syrian Christian of the third century were to jump into a Dr. Who Tardis and suddenly find him/herself at a modern English parish Eucharist, horror would soon set in at certain things. The Syrian would not, for a start, understand the *book-consciousness* of congregations today. You have to be able to follow everything or else have it explained beforehand. The Syrian would be happy to stand and let things happen, understanding certain parts, content not to understand certain others immediately. I suspect that one of the main obstacles we encounter in our road toward spiritual subtlety is that we are trained to expect the meaning of things to leap to our minds. But in the gospel this is not possible. Jesus took care to explain only certain things, and he was aware of the capacity human beings have to get the wrong end of the stick.

And yet the freedom that many of the ancient rites had with the second part of the Eucharist was fairly extensive provided that some sort of shape was followed, so that people knew roughly where they were as the liturgy unfolded. To that second part we must now turn.

(2)

The words of Christ at the Last Supper lie at the heart of the celebration of the Holy Communion. At one level it was just the story of a Jewish rabbi having a Passover meal with his friends. There is much that does resemble Jewish Passover, with its tale of deliverance from slavery to freedom under God and the fact that the new community both commemorates a past great event *and* looks forward to great things in the future.

But the Eucharist implies much more. Nowadays many different names are used and each title implies a particular emphasis that has been part of the service right from the start. Roman Catholics call it the *Mass*—which means being sent out to get on with the Christian mission. So on that score, the Eucharist is about mission. Many Protestants call it *Holy Communion*—which means sharing together in a solemn act. On that basis, the Eucharist is about fellowship. The Eastern Churches call it the *liturgy*—which means the work of the people . . . as if the Eucharist were at one and the same time something in which everybody has a part. The early Christians frequently called it the *offering*—a reminder that Christ's offering on the cross is celebrated when his followers gather round that table. By far the commonest term today, and one that is being used right across the old divisions, is *Eucharist*, which is taken from the Greek word for ''thanksgiving,'' showing that the Supper of the Lord is fundamentally an act of thanksgiving to the Father, through the Son, in the power of the Spirit for the mighty acts of God in Christ, in his Church, now.

We cannot trace all these terms back to the earliest times, but we find their meanings there nonetheless. Jesus may have been celebrating his last Passover meal on earth with his followers, and that involved a special ritual with readings and prayers and the sharing of bread and wine. But within the lifetime of the New Testament, a tension emerged over the role of the meal in which it was set. Paul came across problems at Corinth. People were gathering in cliques and eating and drinking too much. So the ordinary meal came to be separated from the Eucharist itself, for fear of confusion and perhaps in order to safeguard the distinctive character of this new, central act of worship, in which Christ's disciples were able to experience his presence as they made a solemn memorial of his death. The meal survived as a special "love-feast" *(agape)* in some places, but it eventually died out, though there have been attempts in recent centuries to revive it, and it is common today as a means of enabling separated Christians to have fellowship with one another when they are unable to share Communion together.

For a complete account of an early Eucharist, we must turn again to the *First Apology* of Justin Martyr:

> When we have ended the prayers, we greet one another with a kiss. Then bread and a cup of water and of mixed wine are brought to him who presides over the brethren, and he takes them and offers praise and glory to the Father of all in the name of the Son and of the Holy Spirit, and gives thanks at some length that we have been deemed worthy of these things from him. When he has finished the prayers and the thanksgiving, all the people present give their assent by saying "Amen."
>
> And when the president has given thanks and all the people have assented, those whom we call deacons give to each one present a portion of the bread and wine over which thanks have been given, and take them to those who are not present.[13]

This tells us quite a bit! For a start, the prayers of intercession which follow the sermon and the Bible readings lead straight into a special greeting, which Justin calls a kiss. Most modern liturgies have reintroduced this custom. It was probably a kiss on the mouth—and it later became an embrace. Nowadays it is usually a warm handshake.

Some people have found it hard to get used to, but the first Christians did not regard it as a trivial "hello," rather as a sign of their unity with one another. Several New Testament epistles end with the command to greet one another with a holy kiss (see 2 Cor 13:12; 1 Thess 5:26; 1 Pet 5:14) or refer to greeting or to peace in conclusion (see Rom 16:20; 1 Cor 16:20; Gal 6:16; Eph 6:23; Phil 4:21; Col 4:18; 2 Thess 2:16). Subsequent generations of Christians inserted it into the Eucharist so that it came at the point of juncture between the first and second parts—after the prayers and before the preparation of the table. They may well have used Jesus' warning about the need to be reconciled before placing an offered gift on the altar in the Temple (see Matt 5:24) as a reason for adopting this position.

Then the table is prepared—bread and wine are brought forward. This action became complicated by additional ceremonies in later centuries. In some churches, incense is offered to honor the Eucharistic gifts and mark them off in a ritual manner. In other places, members of the congregation themselves take the gifts to the altar in what is often called the "offertory procession," to show their link with what is going on in the service and to make the point that the Eucharist is about making the ordinary world a sacred place for a new way of living.

After this, the president says the prayer of thanksgiving over the bread and cup. Justin doesn't give much of a clue as to what this prayer contains, although he is avowedly Trinitarian—the prayer mentions Father, Son, and Holy Spirit. In writing for outsiders he has no desire to put them off with too much detail. He does, however, imply that the prayer is lengthy—and is a special one, in which the Church says what the Eucharist is and does. The Trinitarian formula suggests an important area of concern in the early Church that the language of worship should express right doctrine and not move off into the latest trend or sect.

Finally, everyone shares the bread and wine. There is no question of anyone being present (including small children) without receiving Communion. And the gifts are also taken to people at home who are hindered from attending Sunday worship. This is something that is being revived in many places today, replacing a more intermittent ministry whereby clergy have visited the sick and elderly with Holy Communion on a weekday. Of course, the two ways of taking Communion to folk at home are complementary.

Bread and wine have been mentioned several times so far. It's clear that there are many brands of bread and wine all over the world today. Although the Jews used unleavened bread at the Passover, there is no evidence of Christians doing the same for several centuries. Wafer-bread only came to be used in the West during the Middle Ages. Everywhere else, local churches just cooked their own local brand, whether in a loaf or in smaller cakes. Similarly with the wine—and the more sticky varieties came to be watered down. In the past 100 years the temperance movement has encouraged some Christians to adopt nonalcoholic wine, but the early Christians did not go in for that. Moreover, they were told to be reverent in the way they handled the elements on receiving them. Origen, who lived in Alexandria in Egypt from about 185 to 255, once preached a sermon with the following injunction:

> You who are wont to take part in the divine mysteries know how carefully and reverently you guard the body of the Lord when you receive it, lest the least crumb of it should fall to the ground, lest anything should be lost of the hallowed gift.[14]

The early Christians saw in the elements of bread and wine signs of creation, destruction, and new creation. And they linked that with the very truth they believed they were celebrating in the Eucharist, that we are broken and yet one in Christ, that we are scattered far and wide and yet united to him. That theme is taken up in a prayer that appears in the *Didache:*

> As this broken bread was scattered over the mountains and when brought together became one, so let your Church be brought together from the ends of the earth into your kingdom; for yours are the glory and the power through Jesus Christ for evermore.[15]

Perhaps it was this reverence for the creative gifts of God and humanity that sparked the idea, taken up a couple of centuries later, that those who provided the bread and wine and offered them should be prayed for, too, in the intercessions at the Eucharist.

The thanksgiving prayer, usually called the "Eucharistic prayer," has a long and rich history. Even in those early centuries, different churches used their own (often quite distinct) styles and conventions in putting this unique prayer together. It is remarkable, however, that for all the differences, the prayer usually has some signals and signposts. These include the opening command, "Lift up your hearts," and a concluding act of praise to the Father with the Son in the unity of the Spirit. But what went on in the middle varied according to the language and tradition of the worshipers. For example, in East Syria where Syriac (related to Jesus' own Aramaic) was spoken we find in an old prayer that probably dates from the third century:

> And with these heavenly powers we give thanks to you, O Lord, even we, your lowly, weak and miserable servants, because you have effected in us a great grace which cannot be repaid, in that you put on our humanity so as to quicken us by your divinity. And you lifted up our poor estate, and righted our fall. And you raised up our mortality. And you forgave our debts. You justified our sinfulness and you enlightened our understanding. And you, our Lord and our God, vanquished our enemies and made triumphant the lowliness of our weak nature through the abounding compassion of your grace.[16]

That speaks of God's condescending love in coming among us. Some of its style is similar to the Jewish meal-blessings still in use today.

On the other hand, in the *Apostolic Tradition* of Hippolytus, dating from around the same time but probably written in Rome, we find a prayer originally written in Greek that runs as follows:

> We give you thanks, O God,
> through your beloved Servant, Jesus Christ.
> It is he whom you have sent in these last times
> to save us and redeem us,
> and be the messenger of your will.
> He is your Word,
> inseparable from you,

through whom you made all things
and in whom you take delight.[17]

From these and many other local prayers countless more are derived, some in use today in an unbroken chain down through the centuries. Others have been written in our time using those ancient models in order to recapture a sense of joy and thanksgiving when Christians gather to break bread. People see in the Eucharistic prayer an opportunity to give thanks in different ways for God's mighty acts. Some modern service books provide alternative texts at this point. The early Christians had a custom of allowing the president to improvise them according to certain conventions. It obviously meant that a good prayer leader would give his congregation a good prayer. Conversely, someone who wasn't particularly gifted (but thought he was!) might go on a bit and say not very much. That may explain the trend towards standardization that can be seen in the fourth century.

Most of the prayers that have come down to us make a point of linking the Eucharist with the cross and giving thanks for the privilege of offering service to God. This is how the prayer in the *Apostolic Tradition* deals with the matter:

Remembering therefore his death and resurrection,
we offer you this bread and cup,
thankful that you have counted us worthy
to stand in your presence
and show you priestly service.[18]

(3)

Already, then, in those early centuries we can see certain structures appearing, and they produce the raw material for much of what has gone into Church life in the intervening centuries. We can imagine the Sunday gathering in a church like the one at Dura Europos, that converted patio-house on the sunny banks of the Euphrates. On the other hand, it could well be the same sort of service but in another culture and tongue—in a North African church, as the illustration at the head of this chapter shows. The local bishop would be there with his clergy, some of them working in what we would call secular employment. No special vestments would be worn. The congregation might sing a simple hymn or else a psalm. The little buildings were quite unimpressive and formed a backdrop for a range of equally unimpressive services and activities during the week, all of which was a powerful binding force on a minority group who felt impelled to come together Sunday by Sunday to "do this in remembrance of me."

What did it mean to them? It probably meant many things, but certain themes come out of the prayers we have quoted.

One is a sense that Christ is present, both in the reading and preaching of the Word and at the table in the sharing of the bread and wine. They took both these activities seriously, which was why they soon restricted who should preach the sermon and who should preside at the Eucharist, as we shall see in the next chapter. But they were reluctant to *define how* Jesus is present. They would not have understood many of the tedious controversies that ripped the Church apart in later centuries. In one prayer, probably written in Asia Minor at the end of the third century, we come across the following words:

> And we, sinners and unworthy and wretched, pray you, our God,
> in adoration that in the good pleasure of your goodness
> your Holy Spirit may come upon us
> and upon these gifts that are set before you,
> and may sanctify them and make them holy of holies.
> Make us worthy to partake of your holy things
> for sanctification of soul and body,
> that we may become one body and one spirit,
> and may have a portion with all the saints
> who have been well pleasing to you from eternity.[19]

All it says is "make them holy of holies." No vagueness there, because "holy of holies" is a powerful idea which harks back to the most sacred space in the Jewish Temple, long since destroyed. They are refraining from being too precise, as if to say to people, "use your imaginations a bit." Also, the part of the prayer quoted ends with a petition that the communicants should be united with one another and with Christ and have a share in the joys of eternity. Many a modern prayer dwells on the theme of unity almost to the point of obsession, but it misses the logical conclusion of such a cry for God's uniting power. That is to pray that the Church, in being united, will also be united with the saints in glory. Many people yearn for a more explicit articulation of the "other worldly," and the more flat and banal the hymns and prayers of modern churches become, the more people will yearn for richer and more authentically Christian fare.

There is another important theme that runs through these early texts—sacrifice. It is hard for modern Christians to approach this language because it has been a controversial subject. At the Reformation it seemed as if Catholics went one way and insisted that the Mass was the offering of a sacrifice, while Protestants went in exactly the opposite direction and insisted that the Lord's Supper cannot be an offering to God, since it is a celebration of his condescending love (exactly the theme of the Syriac prayer quoted earlier!).

To the early Christian sacrifice was something experienced all the time, with the ritual slaughter of animals at pagan altars. But they were anxious to explore the *moral* aspect of sacrifice, that the Eucharist is not a cozy habit to get into but implies (and requires) mutual commitment, right relationships within the congregation, and Christlikeness both during the service and also when it is over and the world makes its obvious and often crushing demands. The *Didache* goes so far as to make the nature of this lifestyle explicit in the following terms:

> Assemble on the Lord's Day, and break bread and offer the Eucharist; but first make confession of your faults, so that your sacrifice may be a pure one. Anyone who has a difference with his fellow is not to take part with you until they have been reconciled, so as to avoid any profanation of your sacrifice. For this is the offering of which the Lord has said, "Everywhere and always bring

me a sacrifice that is undefiled, for I am a great king,'' says the Lord, ''and my name is the wonder of the nations'' (Mal 1:11, 14).[20]

Can this teach us anything? It may come as a surprise that the early Christians should take forgiveness of sins and reconciliation so seriously and yet omit having a full-blooded confession in their liturgy. But they managed to cope with the matter just as well! In our own day, it is perhaps necessary to expand on that moral understanding of sacrifice rather more than we have done. Too many of our family Eucharists are a bit too jolly, almost to the point of trivialization of the Gospel. Without suggesting for a moment that we should return to doom and gloom and the kind of Protestant and Catholic piety that was rigid and strict, I think we can still learn something positive and divinely real from what the *Didache* is trying to tell us about the way to heaven.

6: Orders and Ministry

(1)

I went to an ordination service recently in one of our cathedrals. The place was packed from end to end with relatives, friends, and parishioners from all over the country. The diocesan bishop presided at the service, which in every respect expressed the life of his diocese. Archdeacons, those curious officials whose ancestors grew up in late antiquity, read the lessons. The choir sang some superb music. Over a thousand people received Communion. And afterward we all went back to our local churches, tired by the length of the service but nevertheless inspired to have felt we were part of something so very much bigger than our own ecclesiastical back gardens.

I went away feeling both continuity and *dis*continuity with our forebears in antiquity. True, the basic procedure outlined in the New Testament that the candidates should be selected, prayed over, given the laying on of hands, and sent forth on their respective ministries did happen. But there was a great deal of overlap, and the dominant theme was that of bishop and diocese. The greater contained the less. We were part of a larger family. The congregation was asked to give its assent to the ordinations and also to give its support to the women and men ordained in their future ministry.

But the fact of the matter is that when I compared what I had just been to with what I knew of the early Church's procedures,

65

the similarities did not go all that far. Ordination today usually is the culmination of years of soul searching, training, intense prayer. It is a deeply significant event in the lives of those being ordained. For myself, it came after three years of theological college, an endurance test in itself, consisting of all manner of hurdles such as examinations, pastoral placements, and a corporate life the like of which I had not experienced before and have not experienced since. If I had to find a parallel in antiquity, it would not be in *ordination* procedures—it would be in the careful way in which the first Christians prepared candidates for *baptism*.

As we shall see, early ordination rites are paltry and functional compared with the fuss and bother made over baptism. And one can see why. Baptism is the first step in the Christian life, and it is embedded in the life and teaching of Jesus. You follow Christ as part of your discipleship, and Jesus told his followers to *baptize* all people (see Matt 28:19). But he did not tell them to *ordain* them!

This is not to belittle ordination. As the following pages will show, ordination evolved slowly and surely as a necessary step toward ensuring that the Christian community, in its central as well as its local aspects, both had some relationship within its various parts and carried on the work of the gospel. But twentieth-century Christians who look for parallels of atmosphere between modern ordination and early Church life would do better to compare it with the hype of those baptismal rites we looked at in a previous chapter.

Another difficulty which we bring to our understanding of orders and ministry is that Western Christians live with varied types of Church organization, all of them expressing different but overlapping insights and inheritances. The example I have just cited fits neatly into the Anglican pattern of things: bishop, diocese, hierarchy, grand service—into all of which the local Church somehow has to be fitted. For this model the starting point is very much the universal Church, set over against the particular Church. (This was a New Testament tension, and one with which

Paul had to grapple constantly at the pastoral and administrative level—it is by no means something new.)

But there are Churches of the Reformed tradition whose hierarchy works slightly further "down." The Roman Catholic and Anglican model consists of bishop, presbyter (usually called priest), and deacon. In the Reformed tradition you have a local Church with a ministry made up of the eldership and the minister. That in turn is part of a "presbytery," chaired by a moderator which in turn makes up the wider group, also chaired by a moderator. The thrust is different. In this scheme ordinations never take place in a cathedral simply because there is no such thing as a cathedral in the Reformed tradition. A man or a woman at the start of ordained ministry is ordained by the local presbytery in the local Church concerned. And that local presbytery will also be responsible for inducting him/her at the start of a fresh ministry. The matter will take on an even more local coloring if there is a Eucharist at the ordination service. The moderator concerned presides over the ordination rite, and the newly ordained minister will preside at the Eucharist as his/her first act. It would seem, therefore, as if the Anglican and Reformed models are in direct contrast with one another. Each has the same basic constituent parts. But the understanding of the nature of the Church is slightly different in each case.

There is a third obstacle in our approach to ministry in the early Church that also needs to be identified. In most Churches today ordination is seen to be for life. That is certainly the thrust of ordination language in both the Roman Catholic and Anglican Churches. But it is a hidden expectation in many other Churches as well. People even sometimes speak of the "indelibility" of orders, best summed up by the expression, "once a priest always a priest." Only in recent years has this been called into question, not so much by people who do not believe in the principle but by a more personal approach to the life of the ordained person. When I moved from a university chaplaincy to a parish, it was a very great transition for myself and (not least) for my family. (In fact, the families of clergy usually get forgotten during these transitions.) But as I keep telling my present congregation, it's not just *they* that have souls to be saved and spiritual journeys to maintain and develop. *I* have to do the same. *I* have my development, my lifelong pilgrimage!

What does this mean in relation to the early Church? It means that we need to be ready to see types of ministry in a slightly more provisional nature, not as subjective ego trips but rather as people growing in different ways, developing new sides to their ministry. Paul manages to inculcate some of this in his epistles where he keeps writing about himself in contrast to the office which he holds.

Finally, yet one more obstacle stands in the way, though many modern developments in the Church today may well enable us to see this matter in a different light. Many a contemporary congregation will have a priest or minister surrounded by all kinds of *ad hoc* ministries and helpers such as deacons, readers, pastoral assistants, and many other besides. Some of these require some sort of training and licensing by the wider Church, others simply require the assent and approval of the local congregation, even with a stipulation that they can only operate for a certain number of years. We speak today of a difference between ordination, which is central and for life, and licensing or commissioning, which is usually temporary. Does the early Church have anything like this distinction? To that we must now turn.

(2)

The three ministries that are often described as historic in the Church are those of bishop, presbyter, and deacon. All three are mentioned in the New Testament, but it is not at all clear how they related to each other. "Bishop" comes from the Greek word *episcopos*, meaning "overseer." (That is why many Methodists and some Lutherans call their bishops "superintendents.") "Presbyter" is the Greek word for "elder." Although the word "priest" is the most common term, it is not, strictly speaking, the most accurate; there is a tendency today to revert to "presbyter," even though there are modern languages where "priest" and "minister" are one and the same (e.g., Danish). "Deacon" is the Greek word for "servant" *(diaconos)*, which is why we speak of the "diaconate" as the group term for the order of deacons.

Alongside this emerging threefold ministry in the New Testament should be set references to different types of ministry that seem to refer not so much to the needs of the community in how it is ordered as to the different gifts that individuals may have. This is, in the final analysis, an insoluble issue, because people are people and they have somehow to interact with the rest of the Church. Such passages as Eph 4:11ff. indicate that alongside apostles there were also prophets, evangelists, pastors, and teachers. That does not suggest a directly hierarchical model, though the apostles came first in the list and we may guess that these are ultimately in charge. But the others on the list indicate that some people had prophetic gifts and were indeed regarded as prophets. Others were geared more toward a preaching ministry, proclaiming the good news of the gospel. Still others helped to build up the local congregation in its pastoral care and in the less spectacular but equally necessary task of teaching and instructing people who were already part of the Christian community.

How did all this fit together? It is hard to say. Paul had a hard time from people who resisted or resented his authority, and he lived with the tension of being part of various local congregations for extended lengths of time and also moving around from one to the other. His ministry was, however, primarily that of the universal rather than the local Church. We have the same today in all the Churches. Obvious examples are Pope John Paul II, who tours the nations of the world in his ministry as leader of worldwide Roman Catholicism, and Billy Graham, the American Baptist preacher, who also tours the world preaching the gospel. The interesting aspect of these two examples (and others like them) is that because of their traveling ministry and the media attention that they receive, many Christians from outside their respective Churches regard them as somehow their own because they like this universal style of ministry.

At the local level, it would be fair to say that these different ministries functioned in different ways. Some Churches had bishops and deacons (Phil 1:1) whereas others had presbyters (1 Tim 4:14). And the tension between the growing Church and the need for order is seen right from the start. This is what the *Didache* has to say:

> You must choose for yourselves bishops and deacons who are worthy of the Lord: men who are humble and not eager for money, but sincere and approved; for they are carrying out the ministry of the prophets and the teachers for you. Do not esteem them lightly, for they make an honorable rank among you along with the prophets and teachers.[21]
>
> Reprove one another, but peaceably and not in hot blood, as you are told in the Gospel. But have no converse with anyone who has done his neighbor an injury; let that man not hear a single word from you until he repents.
>
> In your prayers, your almsgiving, and everything you do, be guided by what you read in the Gospel of the Lord.

Once again, the *Didache's* interest in and concern for right relationships come to the fore. As we saw in the previous chapter, the Eucharist must be founded on right relationships—so here too must also be the functions of ministry within the community. Furthermore, it only speaks of bishops and deacons. Prophets are also mentioned as an established group, and further back, when suggesting forms of prayer at the Eucharist, there is the direction: "Prophets, however, should be free to give thanks as they please." That means already what we would call today a "creative tension" between certain officials whose duties are those of leadership and encouragement and certain others who have what we might call "charismatic gifts" and who have the right to make up their own prayers. The first Christians, like many today, held these two approaches together. Two points arise from this.

First, it is important to note that the *Didache* in the very act of writing down texts for prayer was breaking a Jewish convention which refused to do such a thing. It was regarded as too terrible and awesome to dare to give full texts of prayers in written form, which is why the rabbis learned them by heart, and (some would maintain) improvised them according to set norms. So the new religion lets go of the old in its care for sonorous language and right teaching as these are expressed in the prayers of the Church: some of it perhaps resulting from a good charismatic ministry.

Secondly, however, by distinguishing between those who *can* give thanks as they please and those who *can't*, the *Didache* is making a crucial piece of organization! It is familiar territory for any regular worshiper at modern liturgies! We all know the person who cannot make up his/her own prayers and tries too hard in the process. On the other hand, we also know the person who *can* write his/her own prayers but sticks rigidly to the book with its set texts. Here, then, is the early Church recognizing the difference—and making allowances.

In the *First Apology* of Justin Martyr, we heard of the common prayers that were offered after the sermon and before the sharing of the peace and the preparation of the table. Justin, with his characteristic reticence, does not say *who* leads them, although he *does* stipulate that the Eucharistic prayer is recited by the president. (It is interesting that he uses the term "president" rather than any of the "rank" terms we have already seen in the New Testament.) I would hazard a guess that these common prayers were led by various layfolk and not confined to a particular ministry or order. As the people's prayers, they rightly belong to them, the president perhaps introducing and concluding them from the chair.

Just to confuse the picture further, we need to take into consideration the writings of Ignatius of Antioch, whom we mentioned in the introductory chapter. On his way to martyrdom, he wrote a letter to the Ephesians which sums up the gradual trend towards institutionalizing the office of bishop that we can discern in the early second century. The passage is worth quoting in full:

> That is why it is proper for your conduct and your practices to correspond closely with the mind of the bishop. And this, indeed, they are doing; your justly respected clergy, who are a credit to God, are attuned to their bishop like the strings of a harp, and the result is a hymn of praise to Jesus Christ from minds that are in unison, and affections that are in harmony. Pray, then, come and join this choir, every one of you; let there be a whole symphony of minds in concert; take the tone all together from God, and sing aloud to the Father with one voice through Jesus Christ, so that he may hear you and know by your good works that you are indeed members of his Son's Body. A completely united front will help to keep you in constant communion with God.[22]

And he goes on to take an even tougher line:

> If I myself reached such intimacy with your bishop in a brief space of time—an intimacy that was less of this world than of the Spirit— how much more fortunate must I count you, who are as inseparably one with him as the Church is with Jesus Christ, and Jesus Christ with the Father; so constituting one single harmonious unity throughout. Let no one be under any illusion; a man who excludes himself from the sanctuary is depriving himself of the bread of God, for if the prayer of one or two individuals has such efficacy, how much more powerful is that of the bishop together with his whole church. Anyone who absents himself from the congregation convicts himself at once of arrogance and becomes self-excommunicate. And since it is written that God opposes the proud (1 Pet 5:5; Prov 3:34), let us take care to show no disloyalty to the bishop, so as to be loyal servants of God.[23]

I suspect that this passage well illustrates Ignatius' firm resolve to exalt the office of bishop, a trend that may not have been universal at all but one which various pressures, not least the need for unity, exerted on the Church throughout that second century. Something of his toughness of spirit makes one hazard a guess that he ran a tight ship in Antioch. Everything that the Church does must be recognizably in communion with itself, especially the Eucharist. Moreover, people who stop coming to the Eucharist cut themselves off from the Church. You cannot get more uncompromising than that. But reading between the lines, it is not hard to glimpse what may be the reality behind the ideal. Christians then lived in a different world, but they fell out with one another, disagreed among themselves, and perhaps were openly hostile to their clergy. But bishop and clergy are by now emerging as a recognizably separate group, or at least that is what Ignatius himself wants.

What criteria were there for leadership other than the obvious ones of suitability, a flair for getting on with others, and a knowledge of the locality? It seems that some early writers regarded the gift of proclamation as one of the prerequisites. And this "proclamation" meant the ability to preach as well as the capacity to recite a good Eucharistic prayer. It was the twofold roles of delivering the sermon and presiding at the Eucharist that came to be restricted to the bishop or, in his absence, one of the presbyters. But even then there are obvious exceptions. Origen, while still a layman, was invited to preach before the bishops of Caesarea and Jerusalem only to be told off severely by his own bishop, Demetrius of Alexandria, who maintained that such a thing was unheard of! *Teaching*, in the sense of instructing converts in the faith, appears to have lingered on as something often done by layfolk, and as late as the fifth century women were allowed to do this in southern France.

A pluriform picture, as we would say today, emerges from all this evidence. In the *Apostolic Tradition* of Hippolytus, there are definite procedures for the ordination of deacon, presbyter, and bishop, but it must be pointed out that the amount of space given to those procedures is paltry when compared with the fuss made over making new Christians. Nonetheless, a procedure there is. When a deacon is ordained only the bishop lays his hands on his head. When a presbyter is ordained the bishop does so, with the presbyters "also touching him." And when a bishop is to be ordained, he is to be chosen by all the people and ordained by other bishops on the Lord's Day.

There are interesting differences in the ordination prayers that appear in this document. Each prays for the gifts of the Spirit which are thought to be necessary for each office. A bishop should have "that power which is from you, of the princely Spirit which you granted through your beloved Son Jesus Christ to your holy apostles." A presbyter should have "the Spirit of grace and counsel of the presbyterate, that he may help and govern your people with a pure heart." A deacon should have "the holy Spirit of grace and caring and diligence." Thus are expressed the intermeshing characteristics of the threefold order of ministry as they eventually emerge in the Roman Church at the start of the third century. But the more charismatic structure persists even within such a Church order, for Hippolytus makes it clear that a person eligible for ordination as deacon or presbyter who has become a confessor, that is, has suffered for the faith and survived, need not be formally ordained, although he must be if he is to be a bishop.

(3)

The illustration that heads this chapter expresses neatly the collegial nature of the ordained ministry as it developed in the early centuries. Seated together in what we would call the apse (at the east end of the church building, or it could be on the bema depicted in the previous chapter, in the Syrian Church), the local bishop and his presbyters form a direct relationship with each other and the congregation. In all probability chosen from the local community itself, the bishop is responsible for seeing to it that the congregation develops and grows and that the presbyters form with him a ruling group assisted by the deacons. At the sacraments of baptism and Eucharist, the local bishop inevitably presides, the deacons fulfilling their roles too (Hippolytus, for example, gives them several). But it is the presbyters, who are by far the commonest in today's Church, who do not appear to "do" very much, apart from sitting there as elders.

And that is the biggest surprise for us. Presbyters today virtually run the Church. A bishop is a distant figure who does no more than link the Church particular with the Church universal—a difficult job that requires endless patience and tact. He is a far cry from that very local figure who is involved in virtually every aspect of a local congregation. Some would say that we need more bishops. Others would say that ordination itself constitutes the biggest obstacle to the Church's growth because it deskills the laity. It would seem that because of the historic nature of our institutions today, we are in danger of losing out on the needs of the local Church. That is the enduring lesson which those first Christians can teach us.

They can also reassure us that the most important task of local leadership, whether by bishop, presbyter, minister, or moderator, is *unity*. Not an inward-looking holy huddle of mutual togetherness, the sacred ghetto of the doctrinally "sound," but rather that dynamic picture of unity that the New Testament teaches us should be our goal.

7: Marriage

(1)

The scene is a medieval parish church on a Saturday afternoon. The sun is shining, the town traffic system is up to the gunwales, the professional photographers are out in force, the bells are ringing, and a wedding is about to take place. The bride and groom have probably hardly ever been to church. They have been living together for some time, partly out of conviction that they need to discover if they are compatible, partly out of the sheer fact that they are products of the age that takes this for granted. Before arranging to see the local priest, they have booked the place for the reception, carefully timing the wedding so that it takes place in the early afternoon so the guests won't expect a large (and costly) meal to be provided.

The priest waits for the bride, and does his best to feel involved with the occasion. He is no cynic, but he is a realist. By law, he cannot refuse the wedding, since one of the partners on paper fulfills the legal prerequisites of residence. Nor does he particularly want to. When the couple came to see him, they struck him as a pleasant and serious pair. Pleasant because they were thoughtful (they didn't keep ringing up at awkward times) and serious because they spoke of marriage as a critical step in their own development as persons, not to be undertaken lightly or superficially. They are just the sort of couple who will work to pay off their mortgage and might return to church as their children (when they appear) start growing up.

It's a cozy little scene. Many other far less cozy ones can be described, like the best man who is propping up the groom because they've both had a little too much to drink. Or the bride who is deliberately late because she might want to upset as many people as possible. Or the wedding where neither of the parents will speak to each other and you can cut the air with a knife. But whether cozy or not, the basic scheme is the norm for many weddings in the Western Churches today. And somehow the local church has to make twenty-five tightly packed minutes in a church building on a Saturday afternoon carry far more than it is meant to.

Marriage really is the joker in the pack, because unlike baptism, Eucharist, and the other services of the Church, most people—even if they are atheists—will want to do something at their wedding by way of ritual, down to the shortest time available at the registry office and the reception afterward. Moreover, even in post-Christendom society, thousands still want to come to church because they won't feel married until something in the way of ritual has been gone through, lovingly and excitingly. For many of them, it seems, marriage is about creation in the baldly secular understanding of that term. But it sometimes looks as if it has little to do with redemption. The irony of it all is compounded by the fact that, for example, in the Church of England the service in its simplest form is the legal equivalent of what takes place in the registry office. That is why the paperwork has to be done accurately and properly. Marriage, then, straddles two lives, the life of the Law and the life of the Church.

Such a marginalized view of marriage, of course, may not be wholly typical. It is possible that the couple are regular members of the congregation, that they have asked for the Eucharist to be celebrated as part of their wedding; and the service is attended by the congregation that normally worships in that church, so that it isn't invaded by a crowd of people who have never been there before. Moreover the priest and other ministers may well have had the chance to get to know each partner quite well, resulting in a truly joyous occasion: the church filled to overflowing, favorite hymns sung, and even a reception afterwards in the church hall. Contrariwise, one of the partners may be very definitely a practicing Christian, whereas the other is less sure about relationships with God and with Jesus. Then there is an opportunity for celebrating the power and the reality of the gospel.

One of the most interesting developments in the study of Christian worship this century has been the growth of interest taken in it by social anthropologists. In 1909 a French scholar, Arnold Van Gennep, wrote a book which was subsequently translated into English, called *The Rites of Passage*. Taking a very broad view of the ways in which different societies operate, he identified the crucial stages of change in the human life cycle. At these stages, there is normally a threefold series of developments. First, there is a time of "separation" from the community, when the people concerned are marked off by the rest of their group for future change. Secondly, there is a period of "liminality," in the course of which they live a strange sort of life which is neither one thing nor another and during which tensions often come to the surface. Thirdly, there is the stage of "incorporation," in which they are brought back into the community in their new and full status.

Those three stages underline what we can see of marriage both in ancient societies and in the Bible and the early Church. Before marriage, the couple are betrothed and are marked off by their community as persons who intend to be married in the future. This leads into their time of engagement, which is a frustrating time of adjustment that affects everyone who is closely connected with them (It doesn't just affect the couple). Finally, they are married, in public, and the ritual usually involves a celebration meal, and is followed by the couple's being allowed to get on with the business of being a normal married couple, though a honeymoon might lead them away from their community for a time.

Such a threefold pattern illustrates the way many couples miss out on the divine reality of marriage today. That crushed twenty-five minutes in church becomes but *one* phase through which they go in a much wider journey. The advantage of the *three* phases is that they help the couple and the community cope with the stress and tension of readjustment to a new network of relationships. How many couples have to suffer from prying relatives who don't know why they are upset? The commercial consumer marriage celebration today could be a much easier affair if the hidden, unknown, darker side of getting married were to illuminate why those tensions have developed in the first place. Without wishing to talk too readily about tensions (some people create them without trying very hard!), a more critical evaluation of marriage as a pastoral sacrament in this way might enable couples and families to understand themselves a bit more. The trouble today is that most marriage celebrations feed exclusively on the cult of the happy, so that when difficulties occur, they either come as a horrible surprise (when they should almost be expected) or else are swept deliberately under the carpet.

Does the one-phase Church marriage of today reflect earliest tradition? The evidence gives us a rich and challenging picture.

(2)

The Bible does not give us an ideal picture of marriage at all. But reading between the lines we can see emerging from its pages some interesting features. For a start, the creation narratives set man and woman immediately within the orbit of redemption. For example, in the first book of the Bible, Adam and Eve are created together (see Gen 1:26-29). God makes them and blesses them, telling them to increase and multiply.

But elsewhere in the stories of the Old Testament, couples are normally betrothed beforehand. For example, Isaac has to negotiate with Rebecca's family. And when she finally leaves her family, she receives their blessing first, a blessing which is about bearing children. Following ancient custom, she remains veiled before she allows Isaac to see her. Finally, the marriage is consummated.

Later Judaism fills this out considerably. In the Book of Tobit (see 7:9-13) Tobias asks Raguel for Sara's hand. Some blessings follow. A contract is agreed and written down by Raguel. After the marriage feast, the couple spend the night together, Tobias first saying a prayer. Later, a prayer is recited over them by Gabelus which reappears many centuries later in a Christian prayer book:

> May blessings be pronounced over your wife and over your parents;
> and may you see your children and your children's children
> to the third and fourth generation;
> and may your seed be blessed by the God of Israel,
> who reigns for ever and ever.

Secondly, late Jewish practice about the time of Christ is given to us in the Talmud, though this was not actually written down until the third century after Christ. Here there are two stages, betrothal and marriage. Betrothal normally lasts twelve months and it is enacted by a short blessing *(berakah)* after the contract is agreed upon. At the marriage the couple fast all day and confess their sins, and they appear wearing crowns of myrtle, and the bride, if a virgin, wears a long veil as she proceeds to the groom's house for the feast. After the feast the groom recites what are called the Seven Blessings (still used to this day all over the Jewish world but recited now by rabbis). They are so beautiful that they are worth quoting in full:

> Blessed art thou, O Lord our God, King of the universe,
> who createst the fruit of the vine.
> Blessed are thou, O Lord our God, King of the universe,
> who hast created all things to thy glory.

Blessed art thou, O Lord our God, King of the universe,
Creator of man.
Blessed art thou, O Lord our God, King of the universe,
who hast made man in thine image, after thy likeness,
and hast prepared unto him, out of his very self, a perpetual fabric.
Blessed art thou, O Lord, Creator of man.
May she who was barren [Zion] be exceeding glad and exult, when
her children are gathered within her in joy.
Blessed art thou, O Lord, who makes Zion joyful through her
children.
O make these loved ones greatly to rejoice, even as of old thou
didst gladden thy creature in the garden of Eden.
Blessed art thou, O Lord, who makest bridegroom and bride to
rejoice.
Blessed art thou, O Lord our God, King of the universe, who hast
created joy and gladness, bridegroom and bride, mirth and exul-
tation, pleasure and delight, love, brotherhood, peace and fellowship. Soon may there be heard in the cities of Judah, and in the
streets of Jerusalem, the voice of joy and gladness, the voice of
the bridegroom and the voice of the bride, the jubilant voice of
the bridegrooms from their canopies, and of youths from their
feasts of song.
Blessed art thou, O Lord, who makest the bridegroom to rejoice
with the bride.[24]

This is a real blessing of God, and it reflects the style of language
often adopted in these prayers which are so basic to the Jewish
liturgy. The canopy referred to toward the end is the *huppah*
which was held over the bride and groom during the recitation
of this prayer. It was meant to represent the house where the
couple were to live. It could also symbolize the presence of God,
as it certainly did when it came to be used in church in the later
Middle Ages in northern Europe during the nuptial blessing at
marriage. (Canopies are still used in this way in the Swedish Lutheran Church.)

Such a blessing embodies sound biblical teaching about marriage as creative, as natural, as sexual, and as a means toward

building up society. It also sets marriage within the wider context of the local community, indeed of the nation.

It is hard to avoid the conclusion that it was this sort of prayer and the thinking behind it that was in the minds of the writers of the New Testament. Jesus attends a wedding at Cana (see John 2:1-11), his very first "sign" in the Fourth Gospel, and the water is turned into wine to symbolize not just the new religion replacing the old but also the importance of marriage as the pillar on which society is to be built in the new way of life to which Jesus is drawing his followers. Though not married himself, the Master takes care to sanctify it. The New Testament is full of chance references to marriage, but perhaps the richest of all passages is Eph 5:22-33, where the writer likens Christ's love for the Church to the love a bridegroom should have for his bride. He is to *love* her, not treat her as a means toward his physical delight and gratification. The theme of one flesh (see Gen 2:24) is one more indication of the need for unity both within the community and also in the marriage relationship.

When the question has been asked "How did early Christians marry?" the answer has sometimes been given that we know nothing whatever about this. That is not, strictly speaking, true. While we have no definite texts until the third century (was that not true also of other services we have looked at so far?) there are subtle hints and warnings that marriage within the Christian community is a concern of the local officials. Roman law permitted any religion to continue to carry out its own marriage rituals, only making the stipulation that the partners must make their consent. This has been a long tradition both in secular law and in Church practice down the ages, and it is one of the reasons why some Churches can be relied upon by secular authorities to register marriages legally.

But that leaves a lot of room for those rituals to develop and grow, and it is unlikely in the extreme that such rituals did not exist at all. For myself, I am convinced that early Christians, certainly those of Jewish origin, adapted their own inherited customs and Christianized them. Early writers do speak of betrothal before marriage together with negotiation between the families concerned and a contract. (There is ample evidence of contracts at the time of Augustine, in North Africa at the end of the fourth century; and before, elsewhere.) The marriage rite probably took place at home, with a blessing pronounced either by one of the family or else by a local official of the Church. There is the possibility that such a prayer was inspired by the Talmud blessings quoted earlier, or else it was improvised according to certain themes along the following lines: blessing for creation and redemption in Christ and invocation upon the couple in their married life together.

In the (legendary) novel *Joseph and Asenath,* which is probably a Christian book, we have a somewhat comical scene in which Joseph and Asenath are betrothed. They later come before Pharaoh (no less!) for crowning and blessing. At the blessing, the royal officiant places his hands upon the couples' heads. Here is the crowning symbol adapted. We read of it in many second-, third-, and fourth-century writers, particularly in the East, as the expected thing at marriage.

But the clearest evidence for a rite is to be found in the *Apocryphal Acts of Judas Thomas,* from which we quoted an account of a baptism in an earlier chapter. The apostle happens to attend a marriage and the party manage to prise a blessing from him. The text is fortunately given in full and is therefore worth quoting from:

> My Lord and my God, that travelest with thy servants, that guidest and correctest them that believe in thee, the refuge and rest of the oppressed, the hope of the poor and ransomer of captives, the physician of the souls that lie sick and savior of all creation, that givest life unto the world and strengthenest souls . . .[25]

It then goes on with general thanksgiving for what God is and Christ does, and only at the end becomes specific, that is, in blessing the couple:

> I beseech thee, Lord Jesu, and offer unto thee supplications for
> these young persons, that thou wouldest do for them the things
> that shall help them and be expedient and profitable for them.[26]

And the narrative ends thus:

> And he laid his hands on them and said—
> The Lord shall be with you.[27]

How typical this is of third-century Christian practice is hard to
tell. It may simply indicate what often happened in Syria. It does
read rather like a sort of all-purpose blessing that happens to bring
in an invocation that applies to the couple right at the end! On
the other hand, perhaps the writer's intention is to set marriage,
in this case, the marriage of a particular pair, within the wider
framework of God's all-embracing love and care. The setting is
domestic, but in those days, as we have seen, there was nothing
unnatural in praying at home or indeed of having a local official
of the Church leading prayers there. At any rate, it is hard evidence for early Christian practice—namely, that a minister would
come along and give a blessing, with the laying on of hands, at
marriages. A little earlier, Clement of Alexandria cautions against
brides wearing wigs at their wedding. It is the real hair, not the
false, that gets blessed!

Farther along the coast of North Africa, Tertullian at about the
same time states that couples are betrothed by a kiss and the giving of the right hand, after which the bride must be veiled. Like
Clement, he also refers to the use of a ring at betrothal (a custom
taken from pagan Roman practice). He has a "high" understanding of marriage as the concern of the local Church:

> How shall we ever be able adequately to describe the happiness
> of that marriage which the Church arranges, the Sacrifice strength-
> ens, upon which the blessings set a seal, at which angels are pres-
> ent as witnesses, and to which the Father gives his consent?[28]

It is hard to unpack such a rhetorical passage in precise terms.
But it does, surely, allude to the Eucharist (the "Sacrifice") as
well as the giving of a blessing. Significantly, the first item on

the list is that "the Church arranges" the marriage. That is clearly, for Tertullian, a priority.

How typical is this? Tertullian was known as a rigorist about many things. But we may, I think, regard this passage as a fruitful example of what for many Christians was, in fact, the ideal. This is one more instance of the marvelously varied character of the writings we have to use to get some sort of picture of how early Christians married.

In the following century, of course, institutionalizing of marriage services was the order of the day. Interestingly, one of the points at issue was the fact that many people were content to have marriages at home, perhaps expecting the clergy to come there and bless them. This was frowned upon in some circles. Now that the Church was getting more and more official buildings, the hierarchy perhaps thought that these services properly belonged in the more formal setting. But the fact that domestic marriages *continued* to be popular perhaps indicates that the Christian folk custom was embedded in people's memories. They wanted a service at home, and some of them wouldn't budge!

(3)

Do the two pictures, of today's needs and what we know of Christian antiquity, fit? In one sense they cannot, because they are worlds apart. But there is more to the story than that.

First, antiquity teaches us about the origins of marriage liturgy's primal symbolism. The laying on of hands by the bishop or presbyter is the traditional accompaniment to the blessing. That is still practiced all over in the Christian Churches. Then there is the symbol of the crown. Borrowed from Jewish practice, the early Christians in the East took it over, and to this day all the Eastern Churches "crown" the partners during the marriage service. (An illustration of how this might have looked heads this chapter.) Next, the ring starts life as a gift from groom to bride at betrothal and serves exactly the same function as today's en-

gagement ring! By a process of duplication, yesterday's engagement ring is today's wedding ring, and another engagement ring
has had to be invented. Finally, the joining of the right hand and
the kiss are the natural physical symbols that express the desire
for marriage and physical union.

Secondly, we can see the tug of war between Church and
home over where marriage celebrations should be held. Customs
and people vary. The Church has to adjust to new circumstances.
But because of the nature of marriage (unlike baptism, it does
speak *primarily* to the *immediate* family circle), there has to be a
focus on the home somewhere. And therein lies a very complicated story that carries on right through the ages.

Thirdly, the "deep structures" identified by Van Gennep come
back at us to shed further light on the evolution of marriage as
a Church sacrament or ordinance. Betrothal, engagement, and
marriage show us the *phases* which are real life experiences
through which many a modern couple passes, often not com-
pletely aware of them, even puzzled by them.

Can these three lessons teach us anything today? We are not
a primitive society, ordered in a single manner. That means that
symbolism has to vary, though I think that we need much more
than the poor symbols that we have today, with the bride walk-
ing to church on her father's arm and returning on her husband's
as if she were a piece of property given away. (The ancients would
be appalled at that!) At the royal wedding in 1981, Archbishop
Runcie alluded in his sermon to the custom in the Eastern
Churches of crowning the couple and making them "kings and
queens of creation." That would be a bold step for us to take.
Meanwhile, we should make more of what we have, certainly
with the laying on of hands.

As regards the tension between Church and home, I do not
think there are easy answers, except to recognize that the tension exists and perhaps realize that it is inherent in the nature
of the rite. Perhaps, however, today's very stylized practice of
marriage could be loosened up, and the edges of "church" and

"family" blurred much more. The real problem is the departure of domestic *prayer* from the scene and the embarrassment most people (including clergy) feel when they have to pray anywhere that is not consecrated ground. What a far cry that is from the marriage so delightfully described in the *Acts of Thomas!*

It is in those "deep structures" that the greatest challenge of all lies. It is time the Church woke up and reintroduced a catechumenate for marriage in the same way that catechumenates for adult baptism are springing up all over the Western world. It would be pastorally more enriching, humanly more demanding, and theologically more gospel centered. It might also serve to strengthen the institution of marriage at a time when it needs it desperately.

8: Christian Death

(1)

I have spent many an hour at a local crematorium about to preside at a funeral liturgy, or rather (to use modern parlance) to "take a funeral service." The chances are that the occasion is right in the middle of my lunch hour and it may well have been booked by the funeral directors and the crematorium authorities, who might just happen to have consulted the cleric at a late stage. I stand outside, robed in the customary manner, book in hand, as the hearse drives up.

The weather may be "sympathetic," pouring with rain, and umbrellas are ready to be used by relatives whose cars are not able to be sheltered from the downpour. The family arrive inside the crematorium and are whisked straight into the chapel, which is a carpeted building with a pseudo-altar at the far end, candles lit on either side of a cross. Canned music comes over the loudspeakers, deliberately chosen by the family, or else the usual Handel's *Largo*.

The little procession forms. Clergyman and funeral director walk into the chapel, the bearers with the coffin behind. And the service unfolds with its relentless clinical simplicity: A couple of well-known hymns followed by some prayers and with a reading somewhere near the middle. At the end, the congregation gets to its feet as the committal takes place: As the words of commendation are pronounced I raise my right hand to make the sign

of the cross, a gesture which the family may take as a blessing
or a farewell, or perhaps both. Then we move outside to a
cloistered area with a fountain and flowers. The family and friends
huddle together and exchange tearful greetings. I try to talk with
some of them. They may invite me to their home afterward or
to some local restaurant where there is a meal or a snack for those
who have traveled some distance. According to the demands of
the calendar and whether I think it appropriate, I go with them
or else go back to some other pastoral necessity. The whole service in that now never-to-be-forgotten chapel has lasted about
twenty minutes, the stipulated maximum. For some of those who
were present it was seemingly endless. For others it was over in
what felt like seconds, even rushed. And the whole event was
but one part of that trauma of saying goodbye, commending the
departed one to God, and praying for a holy and happy death
oneself. Twenty minutes, as crammed with material as the slightly
longer average marriage rite on a Saturday afternoon. This Monday noon affair is yet one more rite of passage, one of those occasions when people never forget how they have been treated
by the Church, whatever their state of faith. And the most frustrating thing of all is that at only two points in the service is the
clergyman able to "reach" the family directly: at the short ad-
dress (I always say a "word" at funerals) and during the prayers.
And *what* I say and *how* I say it will depend largely on how far
I've managed to get to know the family and to help them cope
with the occasion in as helpful, peaceful, and loving a way as
possible, enabling them to express their grief and their (sometimes tottering) faith.

But then at the other end of the scale, there may well be the
funeral where the person who has died has taken care to lay down
what is to happen with the service. It may be someone who was
a devoted church goer, a faithful worker in the local fellowship.
The coffin with the remains is brought into church the night before to rest overnight. Early the next morning, there is a quiet
celebration of the Eucharist for the immediate family and friends

and anyone else who cares to come along. At midday, the funeral service takes place, having been built up to in that way and arising out of an important pastoral context. When the party finally reaches the crematorium, all that takes place in that building specially put up for the purposes of dealing with death is the committal. The rest of the scheme takes its place in church, a building that is used for all manner of other human needs and cares. It is thus in relationship with baptism and marriage, with Eucharist and daily prayer. Somehow it may hurt a bit less and the full Christian gospel is able to be celebrated, preached, appropriated, or (as we might put it) "sink in." For those directly involved, it could not be more different from the quick, rapid-fire "crem" job described earlier.

But there is more to it than just taking the Church more obviously into view; for, as with marriage, at the human level funeral liturgy *ought* to be about so many conflicting human emotions that to phase it through several experiences like that is not only more helpful, humanly speaking, it is also a means whereby we can "handle" those experiences and bring them into the orbit of the gospel. It is certainly *possible* for the "quick-crem" service to fulfill its functions well and properly. But to phase the funeral through certain stages is, in fact, the historic way, the way still practiced in the Eastern Churches, and also sometimes among Roman Catholics. (It will come as a surprise to some Anglican readers that it also lies behind the Prayer Book Burial Office. But that has long been compromised by secular tendencies that force the service to be gotten over as soon as possible.)

People need time to face and cope with death. And the pressures today are to get rid of the body of the dead person as soon as possible, to have a quick service and get the whole nasty business over with. It's a natural human reaction based on the one thing that pervades modern society—fear. But it won't really do, especially when the drift of modern psychology is to reaffirm the need to phase, to take time, to mourn, to spend time apart from the world. Many are the times when parishioners have opened up to me and said that, although Victorian periods of mourning and their accompanying practices were excessive, we in our day have gone too far in the other direction. We could do with being left alone by the rest of the world, except for some honest-to-goodness pastoral care. But the trouble is—no one has any time. And time, the great healer, is exactly what we need.

Not all the early Christian practices are either practical or appropriate. But they tell us a bit about how we have arrived where we are, what our Christian roots look like, and they also suggest that we could do with taking funerals and death more seriously than we do. To converse with our origins is—yet again—perhaps most telling when we look at parts of the human life cycle that even atheists have to face, one way or the other.

(2)

The New Testament has to cope directly with death because the Christian gospel began life with the death of a human being. The Church grew as a community of the resurrection, a fellowship made up of people who were challenged into a new faith in which death was not the end, that God is able to bring life out of death.

It should, however, come as no surprise that the Gospel narratives of Jesus' death and resurrection should be made up of snippets from Jewish burial customs. In Luke's narrative, the women bring spices to the tomb so that they can embalm the body of Jesus (see Luke 24:1); this was not done first, when Jesus was buried, because of fear of the authorities and the Sabbath rules against work. Jesus' body was wrapped in a linen cloth, according to Jewish practice. The Fourth Gospel has a slightly different version: The body is wrapped in linen *bands*, which already had spices placed between them, by Joseph of Arimathea and Nicodemus (see John 19:38ff.).

In other parts of the New Testament we get little direct evidence. In Luke's account of the raising of the widow of Nain's son (see Luke 7:11-17), a considerable crowd forms a procession to the place of burial. Stephen was buried in a perfunctory manner after his martyrdom, perhaps for reasons connected with the manner of his death—the Jews enraged against the Christians (see Acts 8:2), but his last words, "Lord Jesus, receive my spirit," put the Christian seal on a tragic end. Christian death means entry into a new life, something which not all Jews took to be the case. Moreover, by committing himself to Jesus, Stephen is identifying himself with Jesus as his savior, and by dying for the new faith he identifies his own way of ending his human life with Jesus' crucifixion. Stephen is often described as the first martyr ("martyr" means "witness"), and the effect of persecution on the early Church placed people like Stephen in high repute. Today, in a very different world, martyrdom is still known—and revered. Archbishop Romero is but one example of a Christian leader standing up for his beliefs and being prepared to suffer for them. That context makes their funeral liturgies particularly poignant, particularly triumphant, particularly tragic.

Jewish customs were strictly codified. Burial was one of the most important religious obligations. Dead bodies were regarded as unclean and had therefore to be disposed of in a decent manner before anyone was allowed to carry out any other religious duties. In the Talmud there is a list of things a man must not do: "He is forbidden to do work, to bathe, or anoint himself, to have [marital] intercourse, or don sandals; he is forbidden to read [from the sacred Scriptures]. If, however, the public have need of him, he need not abstain." Mourning was phased carefully. Three days of weeping were followed by four days of abstaining from work and any personal care or adornment; these were in turn followed by three weeks (or so) of formal mourning. But although this may seem to us heavy going, it is balanced by other requirements. Funeral processions were to give way to bridal processions because death must give way to life. After preparing the body for burial, there follows the burial itself. The most ancient parts of this service are not known in detail, but one element is thought to go back to the earliest times. It is the *Kaddish*—the prayer for the departed that is said again and again for dead Jews, particularly in our own century for the millions who were put into the gas chambers of the Second World War. Because it is so memorable, it is worth quoting in full:

> Exalted and hallowed be his great name
>> in the world which he created according to his will.
>
> May he let his kingdom rule
>> in your lifetime and in your days and in the lifetime
>> of the whole house of Israel, speedily and soon.
>
> Praised be his great name from eternity to eternity.
>
> And to this say: Amen.[29]

Originally, this prayer was intended to look forward to the final establishment of God's kingdom upon earth, but it came in time to be a prayer for the rising of the dead to life eternal. It is interesting that a similar ambivalence is discernible in much Christian prayer at funerals. Is it prayer for the end? Or is it prayer for resurrection? Or is it really both?

Part of the present Jewish liturgy includes material familiar to Christians. "The Lord gave, and the Lord hath taken away" (Job 1:21) and Ps 16 form the right mixture of resignation in the face of deprivation and ultimate trust in a loving God. The main themes of the prayers for the departed are reproduced in Christian texts as well. May the departed sleep in peace until the resurrection! May they also be delivered from the everlasting damnation and judgment!

Before we look more specifically at those Christian rites, it is interesting to note some of the influences from other religions and practices that are at times echoed in them. It was a widespread custom to have funeral meals. Among the Jews it was customary to hold this at home, whereas the Romans did this at the graveside, suggesting that the departed needed nourishment for their journey after death. This gave rise to the practice of celebrating the Eucharist at the tombs of martyrs on the anniversaries of their death—their "heavenly birthdays," as these came to be called. But ordinary funeral feasts were sometimes treated with scorn as excessive and inappropriate. Tertullian, never a man to mince his words or to condone practices with which he felt in the slightest uneasy, forbade any Christian, lay or ordained, to attend them. On the other hand, early Christians often took great care to ensure that people who were at the point of dying were given the food of the Eucharist. Ignatius of Antioch refers to Communion as "the medicine of immortality" and the "antidote against death." Several centuries later Communion for the dying is described as "a protection and an aid in the resurrection for the just."

Death as a journey often gave rise to the view that it was also full of dangers from which the Christian should be protected. That, of course, is connected with another view, that certain people are all right at the resurrection but others are not. Michael the Archangel becomes a figure that will provide the right assistance. While this idea cannot really have any scriptural foundation, it expresses the fear that many people instinctively feel that they do not know what happens after life, and they therefore project certain fantasies of their own into this hidden and mysterious world. The hymn from the Roman Catholic liturgy "May the angels lead you into paradise" builds on that theme, and its resonance is found very helpful to many people. Poetry and imagery, it would seem, are essential for good funeral prayers and hymns.

One theme *does* appear in the New Testament that must be regarded as inescapably scriptural! That is the image of "the bosom of Abraham" (Luke 16:22), where the angels are supposed to have taken Lazarus. It does not appear in any Jewish literature, so we must conclude that it is in some way an early Christian notion. Gregory of Nyssa, who lived in Asia Minor at the end of the fourth century, has this to say about it:

> Scripture uses "bosom of Abraham" . . . as a symbol of the good state of the soul . . . . Just as we use the word "bosom" when referring figuratively to a part of the outline of the sea, it seems to me that Scripture uses the word "bosom" as a symbol of the

immeasurable goals toward which those who sail virtuously will come when having departed from life, they moor their souls in this good bosom as in a quiet harbor.[30]

While there is little direct evidence of funeral *rites*, there is certainly enough to build up a picture of how early Christians dealt with funerals. Tertullian may have known of Eucharists at funerals, just as he probably was used to the celebration of Holy Communion at marriages. He also refers to the custom of celebrating the Eucharist at anniversaries, not just of martyrs but of ordinary Christians. This was an important bridge to cross as long as it didn't give rise to a "first class" versus "second class" Christian conflict! Eusebius, whom we quoted in an earlier chapter for his discussion of daily prayer, has this to say about burial:

> With willing hands they [Christians] raised the bodies of the saints to their bosoms; they closed their eyes and mouths, carried them on their shoulders, and laid them out; they clung to them, embraced them, washed them, and wrapped them in grave clothes.[31]

In going to such lengths as these in the care of their dead, Eusebius' fellow Christians stand in sharp contrast to the pagans, who abandoned their dead if they died of plague and treated corpses not buried as dirt. Are there, I wonder, parallels with the practices and attitudes of the present day? AIDS victims often fear that this is precisely what will happen when they die. Anyone intent on behaving like that should take note that Eusebius would probably categorize them as "pagan" in their contempt for the dead.

On the other hand, there were preachers who condemned "rich" funerals on the grounds that Christians should not be out to impress others, and excessive mourning as implying that they had no real ground for faith and hope. Some people left specific instructions. Augustine, who was bishop of Hippo in North Africa at the end of the fourth century, tells of his mother's desire not to have any fuss made whatsoever except to be remembered at the Eucharist, which she attended every day.

While it took some time before incense was used at funerals, the coffins were often adorned with palm and olive branches as symbols of victory. Once again, we might learn from our forebears and modify contemporary tendencies to impress people with the number and size of flowers at funerals. What do those memorial flowers, so often given at great expense, really symbolize? The early Church had similar conflicts to deal with, and we gather that those palms and olives were sometimes replaced by evergreen laurel and ivy but definitely *not* the pagan cypresses.

One third-century Church order, again from Syria, is the *Didascalia,* whose Syriac title is *The Catholic Teaching of the Twelve Apostles and Holy Disciples of our Redeemer.* It has the following to say about funerals:

> Do you according to the Gospel, and according to the power of the Holy Spirit, come together even in the cemeteries, and read the holy Scriptures, and without demur perform your ministry and your supplication to God; and offer an acceptable Eucharist, the likeness of the royal body of Christ, both in your congregations and in your cemeteries, and on the departures of them that sleep— pure bread that is made with fire and sanctified with invocations— and without doubting pray and offer for them that are fallen asleep?[32]

Here is a detailed set of procedures, at the heart of which is the Eucharist, to be celebrated as part of the Church's care for and prayer for those who have died. The theme of prayer and the departed continues not just at funerals and funeral Eucharists. At the end of the third century, a Eucharistic prayer, written probably in Asia Minor, has this to say by way of conclusion to its prayers of intercession:

> Since, Master, it is a command of your only begotten Son that we should share in the commemoration of your saints, vouchsafe to remember, Lord, also those of our fathers who have been well pleasing to you from eternity: patriarchs, prophets, apostles, martyrs, confessors, preachers, evangelists, and all the righteous perfected in faith. . . .[33]

And it ends:

> Give them rest in your presence; preserve us who live here in your
> faith, guide us to your kingdom, and grant us your peace at all
> times; through Jesus Christ and the Holy Spirit. . . .[34]

(3)

What has all this to say to our faith and practice today? I think
that it says a great deal. The early Christians felt, many of them,
very close to death, as the illustration heading this chapter shows
us. Here in the catacombs, the burial places for early Christians
at Rome, they met and worshiped in seclusion from oppressors
who refused to understand them. Here they were able to maintain their relationships not only with one another but with the
God of the dead and living, who (they believed) would raise them
to immortality together with their brothers and sisters, whose
bodily remains lay around them, like Jesus, "entombed." In our
own world, so close to death through warfare and other forms
of violence, there is a need for the proclamation of the Christian
gospel that while death need not be *feared*, it does need *attention*.
When people are about to die, they should receive Holy Communion if they possibly can, as the normal food of the Church.
They should die in trust and faith, committing their souls to
Christ, as Stephen did.

Moreover, after they have died, the remains should be cared
for, loved, and nurtured—not shipped off and ignored. When the
time comes for the funeral liturgies to happen, they could be
phased in such a way as to make the most of what there is. We
have enough material from the early Christian centuries to suggest that it was in some such way as this that our forebears coped
with the sad parting of the ways that the end of a human life
spells.

But death is *not* the end. Just as the service could include
prayers of hope and of grieving, of thanksgiving and of sadness,
so the most natural way of bringing all of that together is to cele-

brate the Eucharist either as part of the funeral process itself or else as a regular commemoration of the departed.

Many Western Christians of the Reformation traditions may look askance at this practice because they think it's all about being Roman Catholic and is really supposed to keep the dead out of purgatory. Nothing could be further from the truth! We have seen early Christian prayer and practice which show how important it was to express the deepest hopes for those who have died. If we lock out our hopes and just regard the occasion of a funeral as a sad necessity, we rule out real opportunities for growing in our understanding of what God has done and continues to do through his own choice vessels. The very complexity of our feeling in the face of death needs some sort of ritual articulation. That is what a funeral is supposed to do. The Roman Catholic Church today is encouraging us all to see funerals as some sort of Easter celebration. That is a good corrective against the blackness and misery of how some of our immediate forebears carried on. But it cuts two ways. It's a celebration of faith—but it is about crying. It's a celebration of hope—but it is also about human grief, especially if the person who has died met the end tragically or very suddenly.

But it goes on through those phases, so that the persons remembered before God by name in public worship become part of the public intercessions and prayers and thanksgivings of the whole Church. When the prayer quoted earlier speaks of God giving them ''rest in your presence,'' here is the Church on earth trying to reach beyond the veil of earthly things which can be seen, felt, and touched to the world beyond. Nowadays an increasing number of people turn to spiritualism because they want to express some sort of relationship with the departed. I suspect that this is partly because the Church has let them down and has failed to bring the message of the resurrection of all believers into the ordinary lives of men and women when they are at their most vulnerable. To commend the departed to God's care as we await together the glorious resurrection at the end seems the most gospel-centered attitude of all.

9: Time

(1)

As Christmas relentlessly approaches, the local town or village is apt to get wrapped up in a state of semifrenzy at the onslaught of things that have to get done. First of all, the shopping has to be done—and that may mean difficult journeys and tricky negotiating with various shops. Secondly, there will be school plays and concerts that have to be attended—and that will involve getting babysitters, arranging for the delivery and picking up of children scattered in various schools and organizations. Thirdly, there will be parties of various shapes and sizes, some of which bring out the basic ambivalence human beings often have toward each other. This holds true of work colleagues, neighbors, and families.

Somehow—and each year it seems a great miracle—the local Church manages to arrive at Christmas Day with some sort of evenmindedness. Schools have done their best to make those concerts contain the right mixture of new and old, something modern and different, with something good and old fashioned. What is the local Church to do?

Strange as it may seem, the commercialization of Christmas is a very recent thing. We could blame Prince Albert, consort to Queen Victoria, for making the Christmas tree so popular. Perhaps we should stand and protest outside the local department store when the Christmas lights are put up and the canned carols start getting played as early as October.

But the root of the problem really lies in two crucial issues. First of all, the north of Europe has long been used to the mid-winter feast, when, as the storytellers have it, the Vikings simply ate and drank themselves senseless in one great spree. Such a custom survives even to this day in some of the drinking excesses that people go in for at New Year in parts of Scotland. It is to correct some of that that the watchnight services were introduced some years ago, in the hope that the faithful might come to church instead of going to the pub. Some of this backfires on the Church at Christmas and has resulted in many town churches issuing tickets for the midnight Mass, for fear that drunks will ruin the occasion. I have detected a gradual trend away from the midnight service ever since I was ordained fifteen years ago. It has made the Christmas morning service brighter, better attended, and free from some of the nervous tension of the night before on the part of those behind the scenes.

Secondly, however, we have to say without any fear of contradiction that Christmas is *not* the main feast of the Church year. It may appear so to millions of religious consumers, and the way a parish program is worked out may well encourage that belief. But the first feast of the Church has always been and always will be Easter. The Church, as we said in the previous chapter, is a community of faith. That faith has as its starting point the resurrection, the Easter message of hope, new life, forgiveness, renewal, all those very qualities that often get sentimentalized into bogus moralizing at Christmas. As we shall see, the two main cycles of the Church year, the Easter cycle and the Christmas cycle (as they are often called), really grew out of the Church's growing consciousness that time should be hallowed, that in the seasons of the year different aspects of the story of our salvation could be recounted, proclaimed, and meditated upon. So far from being a complex and sophisticated scheme, it is in fact a means whereby people can dwell on certain features of that salvation at certain times of the year. God is too big to understand and so are his unsearchable ways—but he has given us some pointers as to how we can grasp him now and then!

Celebrating time, of course, has not just to do with the year, it has also to do with the *week*. Many calendars still observe the old way of laying out the days of the week by placing Sunday as the first. Sunday should be the "first day of the week" (John 20:1; Rev 1:10), which is the Lord's day, the day on which our Lord rose from the dead. But gradually this old practice has given way to a new one whereby Sunday is seen as the *last* day of the week, for we speak of the "week*end*" starting on Friday night and leading to Sunday. For anyone working in commercial and academic circles, *Monday* (and not Sunday) is the first day of the week. It will come as a surprise that Sunday was a normal working day for the first Christians, who will have gathered for their Eucharist probably at a very early hour, so that those of them who had to go out to work did so without let or hindrance.

But, then, there is another scale of working this concept of time into the Christian program. We saw it in an earlier chapter in looking at daily prayer. At the third, sixth, and ninth hours and at certain others, many early Christians prayed. It was the natural thing to do, since the day naturally divides into certain main parts.

But why this penchant for time? Surely it would be better to do without it? I think not. Time affects people far more than they realize—to the extent that I sometimes muse that my parishioners might enjoy the Sunday morning Eucharist somewhat differently were they to take their watches off their wrists and leave them in their pockets when they entered church! Knowing the time, like all knowledge, is a mixed blessing. But time is mentioned again and again in Scripture (see Ps 69:13), usually in the context of being ready for God's reign and seeing opportunities for serving him and discerning his will.

Today, it would seem, we think differently. How can Christians who live with curious inventions like the wristwatch and time managers have any concept of "sanctifying time" before God? I would suggest that God is very able to cut through the barriers that our culture may put up against him. I have a very good friend who makes a point of not wearing a watch. In some sense, he is a scrounger, because he always needs other people to tell him what the time is. But in another sense, he is a prophetic symbol of freedom. He doesn't feel deprived. He happily laughs at those who frantically look at their watches on railway platforms, clearly able to do nothing about the train that is late! Just because we have different equipment from the ancients, it does not mean that they have nothing to teach us.

(2)

So far, time has crept into our discussion on several occasions. When we looked at daily prayer, we discovered times and days when certain services and prayers were offered, whether individually or corporately. When we discussed baptism, the time of preparation beforehand and the occasion of baptism itself (increasingly Easter Day) affected how the program developed. The Eucharist was usually celebrated every Sunday in the early Church. Hippolytus liked ordinations of bishops to take place on a Sunday. Marriages appear to have been solemnized only after a period of betrothal, another dimension of the time factor. Finally, funerals had to take place at a decent interval (in a hot climate, a decently short interval!) after the death occurred.

Time affected all of this in another way too. The Eucharist came to be celebrated on the anniversaries of the martyrs' deaths, and when a desire developed to celebrate it on weekdays as well as Sundays, it was often Wednesdays and Fridays (the old fast days mentioned in the *Didache*) that were chosen as suitable intervals at which to hold the service. In one of our earliest accounts of the Eucharist, the readings went on for as long as time allowed.

Associations grew up, as they inevitably do, with different hours and days. The third hour is 9:00 A.M. when the Spirit fell on the disciples. Noon is the hour when Jesus hung on the cross. The ninth hour is 3:00 P.M. when he died. Similarly with the week. Sunday is the day of resurrection. Friday is the day of crucifixion. Wednesday is the day of betrayal. And Saturday is the Sabbath. (The Eucharist came to be celebrated then too, later on.) All this happened against the backdrop of a pagan society. When Justin describes the Sunday gathering, he speaks not bombastically, hitting his reader with abstruse Christian jargon. He calls the first day of the week by the term the reader would have understood: "the day of the sun." That is the right way for a new religion that is trying to maintain its life and seep into the society around it.

But it was not all sweetness and light. The first feast, Easter, has a different chronology in the Gospels. The first three (Matthew, Mark, and Luke) time the passion of Christ to the Passover, held on the Jewish date, 14 Nisan. The Fourth Gospel, however, places it on the "Day of Preparation" (John 19:31), and this conflict of dating led some early Christians to go different ways. In the second century, Anicetus, who was Bishop of Rome, had to write to one of the Asian bishops, Polycarp (who, as it happened, was martyred, like Ignatius), about this disagreement. It was felt that they should all stick to the same day. But no! Most Christians calculated Easter as the Sunday after 14 Nisan, but a few persisted in keeping it on 14 Nisan whether or not it was a Sunday. Those who did so probably thought that the other side was wrong or else that it didn't matter if different dates were recognized. As usual when there is a row in the Church, the matter has to be dealt with somehow.

Easter, however, was little like what we know today. There was no Holy Week to speak of. Early Christians celebrated the death *and* resurrection of Jesus in one fell swoop in a way that we could describe as "unitive." It seems strange for us, to whom the Palm Sunday—Holy Week—Maundy Thursday—Good Friday sequence comes almost second nature. The events beyond those days are all in the Gospels. But that was not how our forebears in those times perceived things at all. They were helped by an enriching use of Holy Scripture. Melito, who was bishop of Sardis about 170 and part of whose Easter sermon we quoted in a previous chapter, loved to employ the Old Testament in such a way as to foreshadow the New. At Easter, he could preach at some length about the connections between the two as they illuminate the festival of Christ's Passover. And herein lies the real meaning of Christ's death. It took place at Passover time and therefore becomes a new Passover. The people of Israel celebrated a Passover that was about escaping from the slavery experienced in Egypt. Christians celebrated a Passover that was about escaping from the tyranny of sin and death. Moreover, they commemorated it not just every year but at every Eucharist, particularly when they gathered to break bread on Sundays. But the Jewish influence was strong, and the new religion was to be rooted in history, in facts, in events that people could look back to as formative. An annual commemoration is a powerful binding force on any community, especially if it is in some sense backed up by a "mini" weekly commemoration. The two always lived in a kind of tension. At the end of the fourth century, Severian, who was Bishop of Gabala in Syria, had this to say to those who might go overboard with enthusiasm for Easter:

> Is there not a Passover of the Church every Sunday? Surely some new victim is not offered in that feast? Surely the Passover is not one immolation, and the Eucharist another? Surely there is not one beautiful mystery in the Passover, and then another one on Sunday, and Wednesday and Friday? For as often as you make the memorial of the passion of Christ, you make Passover.[35]

Here is evidence not just for a popular annual Easter but also for a celebration of the Eucharist on Sundays and also on Wednesdays and Fridays.

But having established a popular Easter, there was also a time of preparation beforehand. This varied from place to place. The *Didascalia*, which we quoted in the previous chapter about funeral procedures, states that there should be a six-day fast before Easter.

It was not until the fourth century that the forty days begin to emerge as a unit. But that is another story, to do with a flowering Church enjoying freedom and expanding her wings. For those first three centuries, the pre-Easter fast was probably slow in beginning, though those to be baptized would certainly have looked forward to Easter with great anticipation and rigor. That, of course, was not really a baptismal feast until the third century.

The "Easter cycle," as we call it, has always been taken to end with Pentecost, the Jewish Feast of Weeks (see Tob 2:1). For some reason that is not quite clear, there was a gathering of disciples in Jerusalem for this festival, an agricultural one in origin, on the Pentecost after the first Easter (see Acts 2:1ff.). What then happened was unexpected, as it was a radical upturning of any lingering associations with the meaning of the old Jewish festival. The Holy Spirit was given to the Church, the gift of the ascended Christ. It seems that just as the early Christians kept Passover as a death-resurrection feast, so Pentecost was about ascension and the giving of the Spirit. (That is, until the separate day of Ascension was introduced in the fourth century.) Tertullian mentions it, as do others. Extending Easter in this way served to link both feasts together as if they were really about the identity of the Church. For those of us who observe a full-blown Church year this primitive arrangement is both refreshingly simple and evangelistically direct. This was the foundation of the later Church year, and it is easy to see how the collective memory of generations of Christians would see, back in this simple cycle, the kernel of the gospel. Everything is there that is of any importance. The gospel community began its life under the shadow of the cross and with faith in the truth that God had raised Jesus from the dead. As a consequence of this faith, the Spirit had been given to the Church, the Spirit that would enable the community to function in the way Jesus intended, to preach and to heal, to renew and to forgive.

All else that we know of in the intervening centuries is derivative. The fourth century, with its impressive buildings and more elaborate forms of worship, turned that simple outline into the basis for what we know today. Christmas probably owed its life not as an antidote to a pagan Roman festival (as used to be thought) but because December 25 is nine months from March 25, which according to some calculations, was the original date of the resurrection. Whatever the precise motivations of that calculation, to keep the birth of Christ on that day brought with it another scheme in embryo. Just as the fast before Easter became the season of Lent to prepare for Easter, so Christmas grew its own preparatory time soon to be called "Advent," a joyous time to look forward to Christmas and also to look forward to the end of the world.

That note is mainly absent from contemporary spirituality. We have become so concerned with making the world a better place that we no longer see it under judgment, precariously poised all the time between this world and the next. Our capacity for self-destruction doesn't seem to have made us any the wiser. Advent today has gotten lost under the trappings of Christmas, and some places of education have to hold their carol services even before Advent properly gets under way. In parts of the Church in the Middle Ages Advent lasted not four weeks but six. That, however, is another question.

(3)

To us twentieth-century citizens, beleagured by the commercial midwinter festival of paganism, what does all this have to say?

First of all, it says that all time belongs to God and not to us. There is a sort of grudging reluctance to let go of our time partly because we are so full of things to do, in the same way that we grudgingly hand over our bread, wine, and money to God at the Eucharist, careful to package the deal in ice-cream-like wafers, sweet sticky red wine no one in their right minds would drink socially, and cash that is gift-wrapped in planned giving envelopes. I exaggerate—to make a point. *We* have to repackage *our* use of time so that God can, in fact, get through to us more easily. *We* are the ones who have put the barriers up.

Secondly, in the rush of a full life it should be necessary to see God there as well, in the disturbance, even if that disturbance happens to come in the most cruel way, like the firm that issues its layoff notices with the Christmas cards. It is important to let God be God. He is God of the living and the dead, of the busy and the leisured, of the employed and the unemployed. The scheme of a daily, weekly, and annual rhythm is about making oases, even if they are very short and small, for God to keep coming at us so that we can keep digesting what he is trying to say to us. I am glad for Holy Week, but certain things have happened in my life that make me, at times, more ready for an Easter that still lives in Good Friday; another year it may be very different. But that is the sort of animals we are. Perhaps we should be grateful that the Easter cycle has not (yet?) gotten its share of commercialism in anything like the fashion of Christmas.

Thirdly, I think that the Christmas cycle needs to be seen for what it is—subsidiary and secondary. The infancy narratives only appear in two of the Gospels, whereas the passion appears in all four and takes up a proportionately greater part than any other theme or episode in the pages of the New Testament. There is more about the events leading up to and including the crucifixion in the four Gospels than anything else. That shouldn't make us dismissive of the birth narratives. Jesus was a historical human being, therefore he must have been born, had a childhood, and grown up. Matthew and Luke explore this feature of Jesus' life in a way that is not the concern of Mark and John. But perhaps the circumstances of that birth could be linked with the Easter cycle rather more. In a previous chapter we spoke about the need for the *ambiguity* of marriage, with its rhythms of disturbance as well as joy. So with Christmas. The baby born in the manger isn't born for a perfectly trouble-free existence. The very nature of the surroundings are about the judgment he will bring, nowhere more clearly shown than in that tantalizing scene in the Temple when the young child is presented to God; and two representatives of the old Israel, Simeon and Anna, give thanks for the gift of God in Jesus, Simeon mixing his prophecy with tragedy (see Luke 2:22-40). Without wanting for a moment to be a kill-joy, I think it's time more preachers explored the *reality* of Christ and preached the *gospel* to what is a pagan world, some of it waiting for good news. Then, having preached our piece, we leave it to God (not the Church) to do the judging!

Finally, there is a timely symbol that has survived centuries, the lighting of lamps at evening prayer. We have alluded to it already. It is the origin of so many uses of candles in Christian folk ritual, and it suits the north of Europe's temperament. In the *Apostolic Tradition* of Hippolytus, the lighting of the evening lamps takes the following form:

> When the bishop is present, and evening has come, a deacon brings in a lamp; and standing in the midst of all the faithful who are present, he shall give thanks . . . .
>
> We give you thanks, Lord, through your Son Jesus Christ our Lord, through whom you have shone upon us and revealed to us the inextinguishable light. So when we have completed the length of the day and have come to the beginning of the night, and have satisfied ourselves with the light of day which you created for our satisfying; and since now through your grace we do not lack the light of evening, we praise and glorify you through your Son Jesus Christ our Lord, through whom be glory and power and honor to you with the holy Spirit, both now and always and to the ages of ages.[36]

That prayer says it in a nutshell. (Others like it have been written in our day for different times and seasons and appear in the new *Book of Alternative Services* of the Anglican Church in Canada.) Here is God discerned, celebrated, and glorified in the gifts of nature and grace. Here is time sanctified and known at its most basic in the lighting and sharing of a lamp. Evening comes, but God is still with us. Lights shine around us, indicating that the darkness is not dark with the light of Christ shining through the night. That is the experience of those who try to take the risk of faith, seeing in all around the hand of God leading his people through the night, waiting for the glory of the fullness of his coming at the end of time.

10: Conclusion

(1)

Charles Gore was one of the greatest writers and theologians of the first few decades of this century in the English-speaking world. He once wrote a maxim that I have always held dear: "There is a special vocation for scholars, and this vocation lies in great part in purging the current tradition, or enlarging it, by perpetual recurrence to the divine originals." Far be it from me to suggest that the material we have sifted through in this rapid survey of worship in the first three centuries has involved us in "originals" that are necessarily "divine." But it will have posed for each person who cares to look different challenges. At the risk of repeating certain themes, let us ask what some of these challenges might be. Going down the chapter headings of this little book, they might be as follows:

1. The early Church cannot answer today's problems, but there are certain uncanny similarities between our own age and theirs. Closer attention will bring these to the surface as long as we get rid of one or two obstacles.

2. Daily prayer has declined in the Church today and it is in danger of being a burdensome activity for the clergy. The first Christians prayed naturally and simply at certain times and hours with short, memorable psalms and prayers. That method might help change a few attitudes and give daily prayer back to the laity. That's where it belongs!

3. Baptism is the subject of much controversy today. There are tensions about policy, age, admission to Communion. The first Christians were by no means uniform in their practice, but they prized baptism as a precious gift, not a routine. Somehow, in our different circumstances, we need to bring back some of that wonder and excitement, most importantly of all by bringing baptism back into the corporate consciousness of the *whole* Church. As long as it lives on the margins, it will stay there.

4. The Eucharist was clearly practiced in varying circumstances in antiquity. But the importance of the readings and preaching of the Word and the seriousness of the prayers come through as an ideal. In an age that is losing its confidence in words, we have the terrible temptation before us of trivializing all three main ingredients. We should guard against this at all costs and regain our confidence in speaking of the things of God.

5. The table of the Lord's Supper was decked with many different nationalities; unity and diversity lived side by side. But in our desire today to resolve old tensions between the Churches, hasn't something of this diversity gone? We should perhaps explore in particular how we can revitalize that ancient but very contemporary theme of sacrifice and apply it to *ourselves*.

6. Today we are getting into a muddle about ministry. We speak of ministries right, left, and center. New forms of ministry often start life as exciting and innovative and then soon become institutionalized. This can be compared with the early Church's tension between prophets with charismatic abilities and more conventional officials. Perhaps we need to discover ways of holding these two tendencies together, stifling neither, encouraging both.

7. Marriage today is in danger of being taken over by outside influences, so that, like baptism, it will continue to live on the margins. A better understanding of preparing for marriage and what marriage itself can do to the partners and their families and friends might enable us to renew its practice, perhaps introducing new symbols.

8. Death, likewise, is migrating to the edges of Christian experience and needs to be brought back and accepted. The early
Christians, unlike some of their pagan contemporaries, took it
very seriously, even celebrating the Eucharist at funerals. Prayer
for the departed is not something to be feared—rather it is right
and proper, provided that it does not judge!

9. Time is precious and often wasted. But even the wastage is
potentially in God's hands. The first Christians brought religion
into time in many invigorating ways, responding to the pressures
around them creatively. If we had more courage and boldness,
we might make sense of what we have, particularly at Easter, the
feast of all festivals.

(2)

But there are three more general issues that the early Church's
worship raises for us. Each helps to set them and us in our respective contexts. First of all, the early Christians were conscious of
their Jewish heritage. We have seen this time and again. It should
not be overemphasized, since Jewish liturgy was developing
rapidly during the formative Christian era, responding to its own
changing circumstances. Even so, prayer patterns, understand-
ings of crucial stages in life (such as marriage and death), and
the Passover background of the Eucharist all serve to make Christian worship an authentic if drastic adaptation of Jewish origins.
That much needs to be said again and again today, particularly
as a lot of our new liturgies owe some of their inspiration to our
better knowledge of this era. It could also help improve relations
between Christians and Jews.

Secondly, the early Christians had to handle an evolving understanding of their own teaching. Theology doesn't come down
from heaven like a flash of light, even though high points of spiritual experience clearly lie behind much of what we have been
looking at in this book. Passover becomes Eucharist, and flavors
of fellowship and sacrifice transmute into a new, evolving set of

beliefs. Death is not the end, so the dead sleep in Christ until the general resurrection. But all of that—and much more—needs time to be articulated, particularly in so subtle an area as liturgical prayer. We should not be surprised that it takes time for liturgical prayer to be brought to birth, nor should we be taken aback that it should change according to circumstances. Greek, Syriac, Latin, and many others are the languages of the first Christians. Their world and our world are not *that* far apart.

Thirdly, unity appears again and again as the goal toward which Christian life should be aimed. Not because someone says we should but because it lies at the heart of what the gospel is about, a God who is one, redeeming a world that is *not yet* one. Because of the gap between the vision and the reality, a lot of time and energy has to be spent keeping in touch with one another; for example, knowing when Christians in Asia are keeping Easter and trying to understand why it's different from the folk in Rome. That often brings conflict, and hotheaded bishops convinced that they are right (such as Cyprian of Carthage hectoring the Pope, as he did!) are not always the most helpful characters to have around. Such is the nature of the community we are. When the Lambeth Conference debates the possibility of Anglican bishops being women and this causes consternation, we must not idealize the early Church into prefection. They had their problems—and their differences—and we may be sure many of these came to a head in worship.

(3)

If any of the foregoing is of any importance to today's Church, then we clearly have a mammoth task on our hands in all the Churches in looking critically at many of the things we sometimes do without really thinking. Perhaps the really "divine originals" are at work already, challenging us from our sloth and calling us out of darkness into a marvelous future. This side of eternity, of course, none of our worship will be perfect. But that is no excuse for putting up with the third rate, the unreal, the lifeless. If in the process we can worship God in Spirit as well as in truth, then we will have gone a long way toward honoring him with our worship and our lives.

Notes

1. Ignatius, "To the Romans" 4, *Early Christian Writings* (Penguin Classics, 1987) 86.

2. "Didache" 8, *Early Christian Writings*, 194.

3. Hippolytus, "Apostolic Tradition" 41, in Geoffrey Cuming, *Hippolytus—A Text for Students*, Grove Liturgical Study (Grove Books, 1976) 29ff., © K. W. Stevenson.

4. *Ibid.*

5. *Ibid.*

6. Eusebius, from George Guiver, *Company of Voices* (SPCK, 1988) 223ff.

7. Geoffrey Lampe, *God as Spirit* (Oxford: Clarendon Press, 1977) 192.

8. "Didache" 7, *Early Christian Writings*, 194.

9. W. Wright, *Apocryphal Acts of the Apostles* (London, 1871. No copyright).

10. Justin, "First Apology" 67, in R. C. D. Jasper and G. J. Cuming, *The Prayers of the Eucharist Early and Reformed* (N. Y.:Pueblo, 1987) 29ff., © K. W. Stevenson.

11. "Melito of Sardis, Paschal Homily," *The Paschal Mystery: Ancient Liturgies and Patristic Texts*, ed. A. Hamman, English editorial supervisor, Thomas Halton (Staten Island, N. Y.: Alba House) 33ff.

12. Roman Catholic Good Friday rite, 1970 Missal.

13. Justin, "First Apology" 65, in Jasper/Cuming *The Prayers of the Eucharist*, 28.

14. Origen, "Homily on Exodus" 13.3, in Henry Bettenson, *The Early Christian Fathers* (Oxford University Press, 1969) 249.

15. "Didache" 9, in Jasper/Cuming, *The Prayers of the Eucharist*, 23.

16. "Anaphora of Addai and Mari," in B. D. Spinks, *Addai and Mari—The Anaphora of the Apostles: A Text for Students* (Grove Liturgical Study 24, Grove Books, 1980) 16.

17. Hippolytus, "Apostolic Tradition" 4, in *Eucharistic Prayer of Hippolytus Text for Consultation* (Washington: International Commission on English in the Liturgy, 1983) 8.

18. *Ibid.*

19. "Anaphora of Basil of Caesarea," in Jasper/Cuming, *The Prayers of the Eucharist*, 71.

20. "Didache" 14, *Early Christian Writings*, 197.

21. "Didache" 15, *Early Christian Writings*, 197.

22. Ignatius, "To the Ephesians" 4 and 5, *Early Christian Writings*, 62.

23. *Ibid.*

24. Jewish blessings, from old prayer books.

25. Wright, *Apocryphal Acts of the Apostles*.

26. *Ibid.*

27. *Ibid.*

28. Tertullian, *Ad Uxorem* 2:8, trans. K. W. Stevenson.

29. Jewish Kaddish, from old books.

30. Gregory of Nyssa, "On the Soul and Resurrection," in Geoffrey Rowell, *The Liturgy of Christian Burial* (Alcuin Club Collections 59, SPCK, 1977) 18.

31. Eusebius, "Ecclesiastical History" 7:22, 9, in Rowell, *The Liturgy of Christian Burial*, 20.

32. Rowell, *The Liturgy of Christian Burial*, 25ff.

33. "Anaphora of Basil of Caesarea," in Jasper/Cuming, *The Prayers of the Eucharist*, 172.

34. *Ibid.*

35. Severian of Gabala, *Sermons*, trans. K. W. Stevenson.

36. Hippolytus, "Apostolic Tradition" 25, in Cuming, *Hippolytus—A Text for Students*, 23.